W9-BWS-007

SHERLOCK HOLMES
MY LIFE AND CRIMES

OTHER SHERLOCK HOLMES BOOKS BY MICHAEL HARDWICK

The Private Life of Dr Watson
Prisoner of the Devil

(WITH MOLLIE HARDWICK)

The Sherlock Holmes Companion
Sherlock Holmes Investigates
The Man who was Sherlock Holmes
The Private Life of Sherlock Holmes
Four Sherlock Holmes Plays
Four More Sherlock Holmes Plays
The Game's Afoot (plays)
The Hound of the Baskervilles &
other Sherlock Holmes Plays

SHERLOCK HOLMES
MY LIFE AND CRIMES

MICHAEL HARDWICK

DOUBLEDAY & COMPANY, INC.
GARDEN CITY, NEW YORK
1984

This book was designed and produced by
The Rainbird Publishing Group Ltd,
40 Park Street, London W1Y 4DE
for Doubleday & Company, Inc,
245 Park Avenue
New York, NY 10167

First edition published in the
United States of America 1984

Library of Congress Cataloging in Publication Data

Hardwick, Michael, 1924-
Sherlock Holmes, my life and crimes.

I. Title. II. Title: My life and crimes.
PR6058.A673S5 1984   823'.914   84-8054
ISBN 0-385-19654-7

Text set by SX Composing
Printed and bound by Printer Barcelona   D.L.B. 23394-1984

AUTHOR'S ACKNOWLEDGMENTS

The author is grateful to Dame Jean Conan Doyle for the use of characters
created by Sir Arthur Conan Doyle, to Dr Montague Cohen, Director of
the Medical Physics Unit at McGill University, Toronto, and his colleague
Dr Harald Riml, for suggestions and guidance of a technical nature (with
which certain liberties have been taken); to David Roberts for helping
overcome crucial literary problems and to Liz Blair, of the Rainbird
Publishing Group, for her exemplary editorial co-operation and infec-
tious enthusiasm.

ILLUSTRATION ACKNOWLEDGMENTS

AKB Berlin 110, 122; Ann Ronan Picture Library 101, 103, 162, 183; Ar-
chiv Gerstenberg 126; BBC Hulton Picture Library 13, 17, 57, 69, 170;
The City and Hackney Health Authority 11; Greater London Council
Photograph Library 50, 58, 169; The Illustrated London News Picture
Library 164; John Topham Picture Library 71; Mansell 26, 102, 161, 204;
Mary Evans Picture Library 29, 132; The Museum of London 40, 43 *(left
and right)*, 46, 48, 72; National Railway Museum 76; Peter Newark's
Western Americana 22, 31; Popperfoto 24, 40, 80, 86, 91, 100, 108, 149,
153, 195, 202; The Stanley Mackenzie Collection 7, 206; Syndication In-
ternational 20; Trustees of the British Museum 115; Weymouth Public
Library 180, 182.

PROLOGUE

———

THERE IS something about the night's late hours – has it some correspondence with the drawing-in of life itself? – which turns a naturally contemplative man in toward himself. His wife or servant (if he is lucky enough to have either) has withdrawn, leaving him sole occupant of the familiar surroundings, relaxed and at ease. For a while he is at one with himself.

A solitary pool of light from his reading lamp is his oasis amid the dark. The silence is broken only by the clock's unheeded tick and the stir of subsiding ashes in the grate.

It is his intended bedtime; his book is already laid aside with the marker between its leaves. Yet the pipe, which has been drawing fitfully all evening, has settled at last into a steady rhythm of combustion. The tobacco's aroma curls, incense-like, into his nostrils, with hypnotic effect. The nightcap glass holds just enough for a final sip, yet not a satisfying swig – and the decanter beside it is winking its temptation.

It is at such a moment that for the habitual meditator all the combined elements are at their most influential. This is the opposite of that dread waking hour at dawn, when remembered fears seize hold and debar further sleep. It is the harmonious moment when, unless he be stern with himself, or fearful of above-stairs reproach, our subject recharges his glass (not too much soda), and settles back into his chair's embrace, to lapse into that trance state when open eyes no longer see, nor ears hear, as thoughts soften into a blur of memories, floating over the events and impressions of a day, a year, a lifetime.

The reader who knows anything of me will be aware that concentrated meditation was always part of my working method. My so-called 'three-pipe problems' have become something of a by-word, thanks to that wealth of detail with which my old friend Dr Watson saw fit to embellish his accounts of my former career as consulting detective. It is not constructive thought of which I am speaking now, however; it is reverie, and I confess myself as subject to it as any old gentleman at ease in his Englishman's Castle, with pipe and glass in hand and a disinclination to make any stir towards a slumber which has never been one of my habitual needs.

The wind off the Channel is in the tall Tudor brick chimney of this snug abode, which has sheltered for several centuries in its sloping fold of Sussex Downland. It is no distracting wind, none of those blusterers which alternately boom and (in Watson's term) 'sob like a child'. It is a steady murmur, sufficient only to breathe the sweet wood smoke into the room. (Perhaps I will allow myself just one more small ash log, to permit the shadows a last dance.)

I am alone in the deep-beamed sitting room. Martha will come in the morning to compel me to breakfast, and chide me for leaving books and papers strewn about, and for having scattered tobacco ash. She will grumble and gossip, and I shall not listen, for that is our mutually agreed routine. She will fuss about for an hour – unnecessarily, in my view, but an insistence on her part which I am unable to overcome. She will prepare and set aside my frugal luncheon, which I shall either eat when I come to remember it, or go out and throw to the seagulls, for fear of her finding it untouched when she returns again at evening to 'settle' me for the night, as if I were some patient or child. She does not cook for me again. Tobacco and a few glasses of something amber are sufficient.

No dog sighs at my feet. Occasional well-meaning folk have urged me to get one 'for company's sake', but I fear I should not give him his due of care or demonstrative affection. I have no instinct for cats, nor they for me; they eye me suspiciously.

In any case, I have no need of company. The old days with Watson, at Baker Street, were congenial enough, in spite of his interruptions and hearty habits. That I missed him during his absences taught me that it would be so with anyone else with whom I might share premises, so that it is better to remain independent of anyone except the likes of Martha, who lives with her snuffy old husband some ten minutes away by her bicycle. People come to see me from time to time. I am glad to greet them, and an hour or so passes convivially; but I am glad when they rise to go, and irritated when they make a protracted business of it.

Had I ever married, I should perhaps be a widower by now, which would be the hardest of all. The facility and success with which Watson has replaced each of a positive procession of lost wives has never ceased to astonish me. They become younger, prettier, and noisier.

Opportunities have not lacked for me in that department. My belief is that, as with the dependent dog and the self-reliant cat, I have had nothing valid to offer. A wife would have found me a sham and a disappointment, not to mention a perpetual irritant, or worse. 'I pictured to her the awful position of the woman who only wakes to a man's character after she is his wife. . . .' Those often-quoted comments of 'mine about love being an emotion dangerously capable of disturbing the balance of the finely tuned mind were no mere cynical utterances, made for effect. It was my genuine belief that those faculties upon which I was all-dependent must not be exposed to the slightest avoidable

The once familiar fireside of our parlour at 221B Baker Street.
I can close my eyes and still recall every feature: the Persian slipper
containing tobacco, the cigar in the coal scuttle, my Stradivarius on the
bookcase beside Paganini's portrait, the basket chair for our visitors'
use in the left foreground, and all else.

jeopardy. 'Woman's heart and mind are insoluble puzzles to the male,' I recall saying to Watson, though he never seemed to find them the least so.

I shall allow myself one more glass. Just one. And while I am about it, I will have another little pipeful, for this one is smoked through. Why is it that pipes draw their best last thing at night? The attainment of some ideal temperature coefficient after several hours' smoking, perhaps? It might be worth looking into – a brief appendix to my tobacco book when it comes up for reprinting.

Here I sit at what, for me, Sherlock Holmes, is the very centre of the world, the Universe. All that I am is here, for as long as it lasts. I lay no claim to possession, merely tenantry. This ancient house, these furnishings, decorations, pictures... these are not inalienably *mine*. I am their custodian while I live, as many others have been before me. It is my business and duty to maintain and cherish them, so that they may pass on down posterity's way, while my body, the nearest thing to being my own, will go the way of all flesh. As to my brain, those people may go on applying until they are blue in the face, but it shall *not* finish up in their museum pickle-jar; while that proposal to attempt to transplant it before my death is both abhorrent, and, totally impracticable.

What remains, then, as my last log dwindles, the tobacco cools, the glass stands empty, not to be refilled? Shadows and memories, and a resigned acceptance. (Will the Almighty – if such there be – receive me with the stipulation that His professional fees are upon a fixed scale, unvarying save when remitted altogether?)

Shadows and memories. Watson, with that able pen of his and demanding public, has given all the big bow-wow details of my career – in so far as he knows them; there is still the Official Secrets Act. I read his accounts when they first appeared, and they stand in pristine volume form on my shelves, never opened.

Tomorrow, perhaps, I will take some of them down and see what they evoke, after all this time. Should they stir some recollections of this and that, I might even rouse myself to jot them down: anything to occupy an otherwise unemployed fellow for a time.

But now, to bed!

The Fellow Lodger

THAT REPUTEDLY long arm of coincidence – which I have found more often in life, as in the storyteller's bag of tricks, to be singularly short – is stretching out already. The first of Watson's narratives that I notice after so many years chances to be that in which he, too, begins in retrospective frame of mind: 'On glancing over my notes of the seventy-odd cases in which I have during the last eight years studied the methods of my friend Sherlock Holmes. . . .'

There he goes with his imprecision! His notes are before him, he says – but he was seldom one to seek exactness. My rheumatic tendency discourages the effort of leaving this armchair, to drag out the commonplace books which would verify whatever dates he is going to pass off so vaguely. I have sometimes thought of getting Martha to move them from under the window, and put them on a shelf accessible to my reach; but I seldom consult them nowadays, and she would be certain to seize on the removal as an excuse for a general 'tidying'. Hooker was right: 'Change is not made without inconvenience, even from worse to better.' For myself, I prefer my surroundings as they have settled themselves around me over the years.

'Of all these varied cases, I cannot recall any which presented more singular features than that which was associated with the well-known Surrey family of the Roylotts of Stoke Moran.' If he means 1883, why could he not say so, instead of 'The events in question occurred in the early days of my association with Holmes, when we were sharing rooms as bachelors in Baker Street. . . .'

It was on the first day of January 1881 that we met. I was taking advantage of the New Year's Day exodus from the chemical laboratory at Bart's to conduct some investigations there. Startled out of my concentration, I saw that persistent young dresser, Stamford, leading in a man a few years his senior, similarly attired in street clothes, with a flushed face and distinctly unsteady on his legs.

I noticed at once that beneath his clothing the stranger's frame would be big-boned, yet lean, if not emaciated. His haggard face was a tropical brown, overlaid with an alcoholic flush. He held one arm in a stiff and unnatural manner, as if it had become cramped from leaning overlong on some bar counter.

It entered my mind that Stamford, whom I had encountered earlier that day, had been celebrating the New Year in the company of this new-found crony, and had dragged him back to what he had anticipated would be a deserted laboratory, with the intention of polishing off a tot or two of ethyl alcohol.

There followed the oft-quoted introduction: 'Dr Watson, Mr Sherlock Holmes.'

I responded briefly, remarking the obvious, that I perceived he had been in Afghanistan. His obvious astonishment at this confident assertion was amusing to see, but he did not question or challenge it at the time.

Stamford told me he had brought this stranger to me as prospective fellow-tenant of the lodging I was contemplating taking in Baker Street. When Stamford had looked in that morning I had mentioned to him that I had my eye on a suite of rooms. The rent was extremely reasonable, but my exchequer at the time stood at an exceptionally low level. There being a spare bedroom, I had conceived the idea of finding someone to share, and go halves with the cost. My Scottish prospective landlady, Mrs Hudson, had consented to the arrangement, but had warned me that I should need to make up my mind quickly. Meals were included in Mrs Hudson's rental of £4 weekly, but my requirements then, as now, were frugal, so perhaps she might be persuaded to make some temporary reduction in lieu. But here came Stamford again, with this stranger, and I took it for an omen.

He looked a decent enough chap, despite certain signs of the incipient alcoholic. His bearing was military – an army doctor, then, without much doubt; or rather, a former one, recently invalided from the Service, for a few moments' further observation showed me that he held his arm stiffly not from barroom cramp, but in consequence of a wound. It would most

The chemistry laboratory at St Bartholomew's Hospital, London.
It was while doing unofficial experimental work here, in the course of
training myself to become a consulting detective, that I was first
introduced to Dr John H. Watson on New Year's Day, 1881.

likely be in the region of the subclavian artery – more a graze
than a direct injury, for he had obviously suffered no permanent immobility. He limped very slightly as he came forward,
in a manner which denoted damage to the *tendo Achillis* of his
right heel. It confirmed to my mind that his serving days were

over, though not long so, for he still bore the dark stain of the sun on his face.

He had seen recent action, then, which must have been in South Africa or Afghanistan. For a doctor to have suffered wounds implied some close encounter in consequence of the enemy's having penetrated to the very safest part of our position. My recollection turned at once to the accounts of the tragic Battle of Maiwand, at which our defences had been over-run and our gallant Anglo-Indian forces decimated. I therefore mentioned Afghanistan, and received a look of intense surprise, but no denial.

No doubt it explained his drinking, which was very likely a temporary aberration, the outcome of a searing experience that had left him with aching wounds and a wrecked career. He returned frank answers to my few questions, confirming that his nerves had taken a shaking. I tested him with warnings of my domestic habits: my fondness for strong tobacco, keeping chemicals about the place, and playing the violin. He countered cheerfully with an admission to laziness and irregular habits, adding with an engaging wink that he had other vices when in better health.

All in all, he struck me as goodhearted, blunt, and perhaps too lacking in imagination to be devious. I liked him. We shook hands on it, arranging to settle things on the morrow.

It is an old, and trite, saying of mine that the ways of Fate are hard to understand. There can be few, except those of the firmest religious convictions, who have not been moved to say the same. The perennial question of whether our universe is ruled according to some master plan, or by random chance, is as far from having been answered definitively in my old age as it was in my youth.

But I am rambling already: what has the working of Providence to do with my having become a consulting detective? I must go back a few paces, and take a run at it.

Having largely wasted two years of my youth at Oxford (Christ Church), studying subjects intended to qualify me for the career in medicine which, in the absence of any other apparent ambition, my father had stipulated for me, I had the misfortune (though fortune would be the proper word, taking the longer view) to be seized by the ankle by a bull-terrier.

*Had I not been bitten by a bored bull-terrier, in the porch of
Christ Church College, Oxford, I might never have achieved my
professional goal. Through the dog's owner I became involved in
my first case, that of the barque GLORIA SCOTT.*

13

Ironically, in view of the outcome, I was on my way down to chapel at the time. I was undergoing a phase of searching for belief and understanding, and my head was full of philosophical argument, but I doubt that anything I might have heard at my intended destination would have settled convincingly the question of whether it had been the dog's destiny to bite me, or mine to be bitten by him, or both, and what bearing any of it might have on the general question of the laws governing our existence on this earth.

Suffice it to say that I fell to the ground in no little agony. The site of the incident was the college porch, where a number of chapelgoers' dogs were tethered, not being allowed within the precincts. The next most boring thing to sitting through a long sermon must be being tethered to a gateway for the duration of one, and the assembled animals were no doubt glad of any diversion. They danced in their fetters, barking encouragement to my assailant who, in the habit of his species, had frozen his jaws onto my ankle bone with the grip and sensation of a sprung man-trap.

Courageous hands at length released me and bore me to my rooms, where there followed ten days' lying-up, during which the animal's owner anxiously sought me out with apologies and sympathy, and assurances that his dog's true temperament was 'as soft as butter'; perhaps his fellow-captives had been irritating him, and he had taken out his frustration on the next passer-by, who happened to be myself.

As one who, by and large, has always found more to admire in the beautiful, faithful nature of dogs than in the ungrateful human race, I warmed to the man's plea in mitigation of his pet, and before the end of term we were good friends. I was never a very social fellow. The team instinct has never been strong in me, and that of the herd not at all. Victor Trevor, as he introduced himself, was more Watson's type; a hearty, full-blooded fellow, full of spirit and the very opposite of me in many respects, yet he proved to be as friendless as I, which had much to do with drawing us together during our years at the university.

But I am making a short story long. What I am trying to set down is that it was Trevor's invitation to me to spend a month of the long vacation at his father's place at Donnithorpe, in Norfolk, which changed the course of my life. It led me into the first case of detection in which I was ever engaged, that which Watson narrated under the title *The 'Gloria Scott'*. Unfortunately, Trevor's own father was its victim, though not before he had witnessed my newly formulated methods of observation and deduction, and told me: 'I don't know how you manage this, Mr Holmes, but it seems to me that all the detectives of fact and of fancy would be children in your hands. That's your line of life, sir.'

It was that exaggerated recommendation which made me for the first time believe that a profession might be made of what I had regarded as a mere hobby, and led to my setting up as the world's first consulting detective. To such things can a dog's bite lead, hence my ruminations on the working of Providence.

I recognized at once that my academic education required a fresh direction, which I should not find at Oxford. Consequently, I transferred myself to Cambridge where I spent three further years.

I came down from Cambridge in the summer of 1877, without a degree, which I considered irrelevant to the work I proposed doing. I took rooms in Montague Street. Its principal advantage was that it was just round the corner from the British Museum, in whose celebrated Reading Room I proceeded to make full use of my time by furthering my studies into all those subjects of science which had formed no part of the University curriculum, but which I knew would make me more efficient in my chosen profession. Every day from 9 o'clock in the morning till 7 or 8 o'clock at night, according to the time of the year, I was in my place which, if it is worth mentioning, was not many removed from that No. 07 at the end of one of the rows which was the favourite of that old humbug Karl Marx. I saw him there often, perched on his chair at such an acutely peculiar angle that I deduced chronic and painful infestation by boils, as proved to be the case.

My range of subjects was enormous and eccentric, certainly so in the eyes of the issuing librarians, who would often raise their eyebrows at the sight of my request slips. I studied the manufacture and texture of cloths of all kinds; the growth of hair; the lore and habits of gipsies; superstitions attaching to corpses; dreams and chiromancy; counterfeiting and the falsification of documents; the trajectory of bullets; the

15

characteristics and likely causes of suspicious wounds; the theories of phrenology, hypnotism, and the supernormal.

All was grist to my mill, and needed study from whatever original sources I could find, for Hans Gross, the Austrian so-called 'father of criminal research', did not publish his famous textbook on the subject until 1891. When I read it (in the German) I was able to congratulate myself on having anticipated him in many departments, although I found no acknowledgment to my work.

I read and memorized the details of all the criminal annals I could lay my hands upon, as well as the limited amount of crime fiction available in those days. I have always subscribed to Freud's view of creative writers who, he insisted, are apt to know instinctively a whole host of things which philosophy and science have not yet unearthed. There was not a great deal to be learned from the likes of Gaboriau, though something from Poe and Dickens, and every little acted as a stimulus to ideas of my own.

Having thus steeped myself in the knowledge which I felt my chosen profession demanded, the difficulty was finding a way of starting up in actual practice.

The methods employed by established detectives, both official and private, I knew to be unscientific and lacking in any background of methodical study of human psychology. The profession of detective in England was less than forty years old in those years of my sojourn at Montague Street, 1877–9; indeed, the Criminal Investigation Department as such had only come into being in 1878, following the previous year's trials for corruption of most of the senior members of the Metropolitan Police Detective Branch. Procedures were not very far removed from those long used by uniformed police, who much resented the superior pay and standing of men in plain clothes. It was obvious to me that much valuable evidence must be going to waste from lack of training in those associations of observation, inquiry and deduction on which my own methods were based. The thing was to find a chance to use and prove my system, in a way which would gain it respect and employment, without having to resort to vulgar solicitation and advertisement.

In the event, I had long to wait. It occurred to me that one way to become known might be to publish some of the more

New Scotland Yard, the Metropolitan Police Office, was the only public building by the fashionable private architect Norman Shaw (1831–1912), coming into use in 1890. Its site beside the Thames had originally been intended for an opera house, which I fancy must have influenced Shaw's design.

original and unusual of my findings in ways which might bring them to the notice of those men in authority whom they could most usefully impress. I began composing some of them, but soon found that writing is in itself an art requiring much nurturing and practice, and my progress was consequently slow. The labour resulted at length in the monograph *Upon the Distinction Between the Ashes of the Various Tobaccos*, in which I enumerated 140 types of cigar, cigarette, and pipe tobacco, with coloured plates illustrating the difference in their ashes. Several of my other monographs, including those on the dating of documents and the tracing of footsteps by means of plaster of paris, were at least drafted at this time.

17

One of the principal benefits of a university education – some would say the only one – is getting known to men who will eventually move in spheres of influence. Although I had had few close friends at either Oxford or Cambridge, I was aware that my aloofness and leaning towards esoteric studies had provided me with a reputation which was a good deal talked of, and the few cases which did come my way during those early days in Montague Street arose from college connections. In almost all instances my aid was sought in default, as it were, by men whose folly had got them into disagreeable situations which debarred them from seeking the help of the official police, while not sufficiently trusting the private detectives who plied brashly for hire.

In later years, when Watson was established as my Boswell, I showed him the papers of these cases, but his better judgment prevented his including them in his chronicles. The one matter which he did include, under the title *The Musgrave Ritual*, was brought to my attention in precisely that 'last resort' fashion by a man with whom I had been only slightly acquainted at college, Reginald Musgrave, of Hurlstone Manor, in West Sussex. Glancing over its details now, in Watson's version, I am perturbed to note many discrepancies in the calculations which he ascribes to me in my locating the lost crown of the Stuarts, in its hiding place deep within that ancient manor house. Had I interpreted the ancient conundrum in the way which he reports, my search would have led me nowhere near to its objective. He even records my having told him that the recovered crown had been allowed to remain in the custody of the family, which, of course, would never have been permitted.

That is the sort of thing which has led to my neglecting Watson's chronicles all these years. If he had lavished as much care on accuracy as he did on striving for romantic and sensational effects, his narratives would be worthy of elevation from mere stories to histories.

I do not think I can be bothered to go on with this exercise in reminiscence if it is to be based on such unstable foundations as a romantic-minded chronicler's flawed narratives and an old man's memory. I shall expend this evening's last pipe over something altogether different – a few chapters of Jean Paul Richter, I think – lest I go to bed irritated.

A Consulting Detective

CONTRITION SUPPLIES my emotion this evening. Having determined to put an end to these jottings, and shuffling the pages together for putting away (the old habit of never destroying a document has not left me), I observed with what little justice I ended by upbraiding Watson for carelessness. Who am I to criticize, having myself meandered away from retracing the course of the footsteps which have marked my career's progress? It was never my habit to beg Watson's pardon, but were he here now, I believe I could bring myself to do so.

The case of the Musgrave Ritual, which occupied me briefly in the summer of 1879, did no more than had any of its few predecessors to bring me new clients. I had thus been a freelance upon the world for two years, with nothing to sustain me financially save the small regular allowance paid me by my guardian, Dr Verner. My Montague Street rooms, and my keep, cost me 12s 6d a week during my first year in them, rising to 15s in the second, when my landlady discovered that her neighbours were commanding higher rates from their tenants than she from me. It would have seemed *infra dig.* to have requested a fee from the ex-university men whom I had assisted, although there was a little embarrassed discussion about expenses and, as diffidently as possible, I accepted a few guineas as a token.

By the autumn of 1879 times were becoming a trifle hard, and prospects getting no better. Something had to be done, and I had Reginald Musgrave to thank for making it possible. He was a very rich young man, having inherited the whole of the Hurlstone estates from his late father, and he had expressed a keen interest in my methods of observation, investigation and inference.

'I must say, Holmes,' he had remarked, as we sat with port and cigars after dinner, with the battered but nonetheless resplendent diadem on the small occasional table which stood between us at his drawing-room fireside, 'you have a rare gift for this sort of thing.'

'The result of far harder study than I ever put in at 'varsity,' I laughed, and he raised his eyebrows high indeed as I outlined to him the extent of my self-imposed curriculum.

'Surely you should be in the police,' he remarked. 'Such qualities as yours ought to be a considerable asset to them.'

'I fear they would offer me none too warm a welcome. I could scarcely call round to Scotland Yard and send in a message to the Commissioner that I am willing to put my expert advice at his disposal.'

'There are other ways,' he insisted earnestly. 'I'm Member of Parliament for this district. I can speak a word on your behalf into the right ears.'

This is NOT *a composite photograph of myself in a variety of my disguises. The men are Scotland Yard detectives about to impersonate a cross-section of the populace in order to keep watch on a gang of thieves, whom they managed successfully to arrest.*

'I appreciate the offer. Even so, I don't think the Commissioner would thank anyone for thrusting me onto him. Once an amateur, always one, in the professionals' eyes, and I understand that the recent move to introduce outsiders whose only qualifications were that they were "gentlemen of good education and social standing" was a total failure. Most of the professionals graduated from the beat, and the rule book remains their guiding light all along their way.'

'Advertise yourself as a private detective, then. Plenty do.'

'Oh, yes. Most have been on the Force, but are retired through age, or injury, or, in the case of the least reputable, because of their own misdemeanours. I have no wish to become classified among them. You yourself came to me as a last resort, remember?'

'No offence intended, I assure you, Holmes. You may count on me to spread word about how this matter would never have been solved, but for you. Your position troubles me, though; you appear to be raising your own difficulties. Depend on it, I shall give thought to what more might be done to help you.'

He was as good as his word. Not more than a fortnight after this conversation in the depths of Sussex he was again a caller upon me at Montague Street. He sat with his top hat beside him on my table and smoked a cigarette in his languidly graceful manner.

'I have been talking of you to one of the Scottish MPs. Naturally, he regards the finding of the Stuart crown as an event of national importance. He went so far as to suggest that you be publicly recognized for it.'

'Oh, come, come!'

'Well, exactly,' Musgrave smiled. 'I told him that you weren't after recognition of that sort. I explained your general circumstances, and how you have equipped yourself for what you hope to do. He grasped the position immediately, and came out with a proposal which, if I were in your shoes, I don't believe I should hesitate a moment before accepting.'

Naturally, I was all ears as he went on.

'Have you heard of Pinkerton?'

'The American detective?'

'That's the man. I was sure you would.'

Pinkerton's National Detective Agency bore an impressive, if somewhat chequered reputation, in the United States.

Acting independently of the official police force, it had thwarted the plot to assassinate Lincoln when he was President-elect in 1861. One of its most sensational coups, five years later, had been the capture of the chief perpetrators of the great railway robbery of $700,000 from the Adams Express Company. It also engaged in political and military intelligence work in the Civil War, and had later earned itself notoriety by infiltrating industrial disputes on behalf of employers. Only recently, my reading had taken in Pinkerton's book *The Molly Maguires and the Detectives*, telling how one of his agents, James

Allan Pinkerton, Glasgow-born founder of Pinkerton's National Detective Agency in which I trained in the U.S.A., photographed during the Civil War with President Abraham Lincoln and General McClellan. Allan, who foiled an attempt to assassinate Lincoln, was less at home in spy work than detection – my own experience.

McParlan, had successfully attained high office in the lawless Irish-American secret society which had dominated the Pennsylvania coalfields, and had secured the evidence leading to the conviction of its leading members, some of whom were executed, and the crushing of an organization which had been growing from strength to strength since the war.

I told Musgrave as much, and he nodded eagerly.

'You know, then, that Pinkerton himself is Scots-born?'

'Now you come to remind me, yes. Glasgow, wasn't it?'

'It was,' he confirmed. 'He was in his early twenties when he emigrated to America. He ran down a gang of counterfeiters, got made a deputy-sheriff, and has never looked back since he set up his own organization. The point is, he and my Scottish friend have been chums from boyhood. They've always kept in touch with one another. He'd be more than willing to recommend you to Pinkerton himself.'

The notion both intrigued and startled me.

'Emigrate to Chicago!'

'It's one possibility, but not what I had in mind. I thought you might like to go there and do, say, a year with his organization, or however long might suit you, and then come back and found something similar here. Heaven knows, we could do with it.'

'It's extremely decent of you, Musgrave, and an attractive idea. Only . . .'

I was trying to frame words to tell him that I had not the means to venture upon so desirable-sounding an undertaking. He gave me no chance to falter them out. Rising and taking up his hat, he merely said, 'Then it'll all be attended to,' and left before I could say more.

So I became a Pinkerton detective, which brings a host of memories clamouring to be savoured. But for the moment, I must hold my memory on its present course, defying the temptation to digress again.

It was August 1880 when I at length came back from the United States, after a little under a year there. My head was fairly buzzing with enthusiasms and ideas now. Plans galore competed for my favour, though the handicap of being without capital maintained an effective curb on rushing into any of them. Allan Pinkerton had offered to license me to set up a United Kingdom sub-agency on his behalf. Alternatively,

A street scene in Chicago, a few years before my visit in 1879–1880 to study the tricks of the detective trade with the Pinkerton Agency. Chicago, so thronged and prosperous now, was then only a growing frontier settlement with a tiny population.

I knew that, should I prefer to create an organization of my own, finance would be forthcoming from Musgrave and friends of his. He had assured me in correspondence that I would find that there was no shortage of potential investment in my talents.

I decided that a period was needed in which I might adjust from the way of life in Chicago to the different style of London. It was necessary to look about me and assess the current state of crime in the metropolis, in order to determine how to mould an organization which would combat it most effectively. There were also a number of new ideas of my own which I wished to put to the test in solitary peace and quiet.

Some of these required the use of a chemical laboratory. Here was a problem, since I had no intention of attaching myself to any university in order to gain access to one, and a tentative inquiry of the landlady of the temporary rooms which I had taken in the shadow of St Paul's Cathedral produced a firm stipulation that no 'smelly experiments' were going to be permitted on her premises. Smells were not what I had in mind, but the point had to be taken. There was also the consideration that my funds were as low as ever.

In the course of a pensive stroll about the neighbourhood one dark evening, it suddenly occurred to me that Providence was perhaps taking a fresh interest in my affairs. My lodging, found quite at random through the columns of one of the evening newspapers, chanced to be ideally situated for my immediate purposes. It was within five minutes' walk of the Old Bailey; the Central London Meat Market was not much further away, in Smithfield; and just round the corner from that stood Bart's Hospital.

Thus lay everything, so to speak, under one roof, for my convenience. At the Old Bailey I could resume my habit of sitting on the public benches, steeping myself in the details of trials for every sort of criminal offence, observing keenly the reactions of accused and witnesses to each nuance of the evidence. At Smithfield, a modest tip in the palm of a friendly butcher provided me with a quiet corner and the unsaleable carcass of a defective pig, which I was enabled to beat with a variety of blunt instruments, and make valuable notes of the appearance of differing bruises produced after death.

Stamford was quite correct in telling Watson that I had been 'bemoaning' myself to him that I could not get someone to go halves with me in some nice rooms which I had found. The fact was, I had made my New Year's Resolution; and it was to accept neither Pinkerton's licence, nor Musgrave's backing, to enable me to found a detective organization. I had determined to go it alone.

Baker Street could not have been a better situation. It had come down somewhat in the world since the days when William Pitt, Cardinal Wiseman and Mrs Siddons had been among its residents, and when there had been no commercial aspect to it, the shops being confined to the many smaller streets running off it at either side. The coming of the railways in the 1860s had changed that, though not outrageously. In any case, I regarded the proximity of Baker Street Station and the Metropolitan Railway as likely to be to my advantage.

Baker Street, a photograph taken a few years after my retirement and departure from No. 221B. It had been a handy location for my work, and lies at the centre of more than 20 years of memories of the companionship and a thousand adventures shared by Watson and myself.

Mayfair was not far away. It was my hope that it would be from that wealthy district that many of my future clients would come – a class of people prone to scandal through the unbending rules of society life and family feuds, yet who would go to great lengths not to expose their difficulties to the police or risk revealing them to the private detective agencies, with their generally questionable reputations and well-known links with the sensational press. It would be easy and discreet for even a distressed lady on her own to make the short journey to Baker Street unnoticed; whereas, had I set up in Mayfair itself, there would have been too much risk of chance encounters virtually on my doorstep, with a deterrent effect.

26

APPRENTICE DETECTIVE

WATSON WITH his three marriages and a boasted experience which had already encompassed 'many nations and three separate continents' by the time we first met, has been at some pains in his writings about me to deal fairly with my attitude towards women. I do not think he has succeeded very well, for the simple reason that he could not enter into the mind of any man choosing lifelong bachelorhood for any reason short of an ambition to be elected Pope. Despite his desultory attempts to explain that which he found inexplicable, he has conveyed an impression of me as a cold, contemptuous woman-hater; and that is, as it always has been, a long way from the truth.

Like Leonardo da Vinci's, my reticence in this as in certain other attitudes with emotional connotations was adopted deliberately and required quite rigorous application until it eventually became habit, and needed no further conscious self-discipline. All who knew Leonardo closely were united in praise of his humanity, warmth, generosity and tenderness. They shine forth from his work; yet the student of his great writings will find them totally devoid of emotional content. He had sensed that, in order to view knowledge objectively, and balance it in the scales against his theoretical conceptions, he had to observe absolute neutrality of sentiment. He cultivated the attitude until, as in my case, it became, not second nature to him, but first.

I lay no claim to being another Leonardo – not least in that I have read that he was not, in any case, naturally susceptible to woman's charms. That was a commoner state in his time and society than in mine, and I know that no such natural inhibition has ever hung over me. I am neither a homosexual nor a misogynist. I do not think the reader of Watson's chronicles will find a single instance of my treating a good woman with anything other than that attentiveness and courtesy which I have always regarded to be the gentleman's duty towards females of all ages and stations in life. My feigned wooing of the blackmailer Charles Augustus Milverton's housemaid was a tactical necessity; in any case, it made her the more desirable in the eyes of my rival suitor, which I daresay worked to her benefit.

As to anything more intimate in the way of association with women, my attitude is summed up unequivocally in that statement which he records accurately in *The Sign of Four*, and which I will set down again here:

> Love is an emotional thing, and whatever is emotional is opposed to that true, cold reason which I place above all things. I should never marry, lest I bias my judgment.

I think it was Samuel Butler who likened life to playing a solo on the violin, and learning the instrument as you go along. It is in the nature of long violin solos that there comes a passionate passage, sooner or later, and I duly fiddled my way through those which I encountered. They occurred in my university days before I had armoured myself against emotional assaults; but it was two late experiences which encouraged me to seal off the last chinks in that armour without more ado.

In November 1879 I took up Reginald Musgrave's offer, through his Scottish friend, to get me into the Pinkerton Detective Agency in Chicago – in those days no more than an expanding frontier village with a population of twelve hundred. Allan Pinkerton himself was in his sixtieth year then. He had suffered a stroke some years earlier, and although he had recovered fully his most active days were over. His sons William and Robert were running the agency when I joined: strapping, active men in their thirties, born American citizens after their father and his young bride had made a romantic and hazardous escape from Scotland, where their activities on behalf of the Chartist movement had made them fugitives from the law. He worked at his trade of barrel-making until he became, quite by accident, a private detective. His reputation grew with Chicago, whose first official detective he was made in 1849, but he preferred to operate independently, and set up his own agency in the 1850s.

It was a huge success, on a nationwide scale. Pinkerton attracted some fine assistants, who went about their investigations fearlessly and in observance of his strict principles of integrity and incorruptibility in a fast-growing country where corruption spoke louder than laws. They beat the Jesse James and Renos and Youngers gangs in protracted 'wars', and broke the bank-robbing Scott-Dunlap gang, known as The Ring. They arrested and secured convictions against the

The leaders of the James and Youngers combination of bank and train robbers, whom Pinkerton detectives pursued relentlessly. L to R: Cole Younger, Jesse James, Bob Younger and Frank James. Jesse James was murdered by two of his own gang in 1882, but Frank retired and died naturally in 1915.

whole of Adam Worth's gang – which I was later able to emulate in the case of the Moriarty organization – and they hounded Butch Cassidy and the Sundance Kid for years. Their operations and branches extended across the world. Their emblem, an ever-open eye and the motto 'We Never Sleep', remains a familiar warning on premises under their regular protection (and, some say, gave us the term 'Private Eye' for a private detective).

It was one of the sons, William, who took me under his wing. He was an ox of a man, thick-faced and dark-eyed, with shaggy eyebrows which gave him an air of considerable menace; as if, in a fight, he would keep coming on at you, no matter how much lead was pumped into him. I doubt that many criminals stood their ground long enough to put it to the test.

He was as affable as he was ferocious-looking, and knew every trick of the crooked trade, which he proceeded to teach me, both in theory and through practical experience.

'The chief thing – well, one of them, for I guess there's no single one more important than the others in this game – is to get to know your fellow men. Most of them conform to whatever type they are, and there are as many types as there are people in a crowd. The petty thief will think and act one way; the bully another; the rich crook who uses smaller fry to do his fronting is quite another proposition.

'None of them tends to act out of character. If you know which type you're dealing with, you'll know pretty well what his moves will be before, during and after a crime, and just where to be to nail him down. Adapt yourself to the company of all these types, so that you can get accepted as one of their own kind, and hear them talk freely. Pick up their shop-talk and their slang and their ways. You've got to feel so much at home in any surroundings or kind of company that you forget yourself and really think yourself one of them. Otherwise, they'll see you hesitate and that you're unsure of yourself – out of place. And once they're on to you, you're useless. They'll clam up, or steer clear – or maybe worse.'

'One should learn to be a criminal first and a detective second, then,' I suggested.

'You've got it. If you have to take a share in doing a crime in order to get your evidence, then go ahead. If you hold back, they'll rumble you. They have a kind of instinct for a cop.

William Pinkerton, the elder of Allan's two sons, was my mentor in America. He tutored me in the concomitant roles of detective and crook, enlarging my capacities for disguise and deception. He is seated between two of his operatives, armed for 'Western trailing'.

Our dad has always boasted that there's been scarcely any instance of one of our operatives giving himself away by attracting suspicions.'

'Surely they get known among the criminal fraternity. You yourself must present a pretty unmistakable figure.'

'Disguise, my boy. The simpler, the better, but what a world of difference it can make. Not to me, I admit. I'm a bit past disguising. But you – now you could change yourself into any type under the sun.'

He went on, in the following months, to show me what he meant. He taught me how to change my face by other means than by just growing whiskers or putting on spectacles. Warts, scars, freckles, birthmarks, the pallor of sickness or long incarceration in gaol – all could be adopted by the appropriate methods and with simple materials. He taught me to faint convincingly, to feign asthma and convulsions, deafness, dumbness, blindness; to limp on either leg; to hold a supposedly withered arm; to dress and walk like an old woman and pitch my voice accordingly.

'Keep a note of each detail of a disguise,' he advised. 'If you're among one mob who happen to join up with another, who recognize your face but have always seen you with red hair instead of the black you've switched to, you might find yourself squeezed between two lots of mighty angry men. Think fast. Tell 'em you had your hair dyed to fool the Pinkertons, or something.'

He added one more piece of information which I have found to be borne out again and again.

'When you're dealing with criminals who use disguises, remember that the expert disguises himself *for* the job, and reverts back to being himself after. It's the tyro who does the job as himself, then pops on disguise later. If he comes under suspicion, and it turns out he's wearing disguise, he hasn't a leg left to stand on.'

I learned to pick pockets, to crack safes, to force doors and windows, to read footprints, to make duplicate keys, to shadow a suspect, and to 'lose' anyone I thought might be following me. At both my universities I had enjoyed boxing and single-stick fighting, but William and Robert Pinkerton and their operatives taught me methods of defence and attack which would have earned a boxer disqualification for life.

They also gave me a thorough training in the use and care of the Colt revolver.

In short, they taught me to be a thoroughmost detective in one; for, as I increasingly recognized, the skills, equipment and mental attitudes are almost wholly interchangeable between the two trades.

They also used me on some of their operations. It was good practical experience and enabled me to gain confidence in my nerves. Fearlessness and a judicious degree of disregard for one's bodily safety are as important to the investigator as are the ability to endure long hours of waiting, perhaps in a cramped hiding place, in conditions of great heat, piercing cold, drenching wet, thirst and hunger. It was all most valuable experience to add to my own more esoteric studies in London.

The assignments took me into every sort of environment, from the doss-house and the speakeasy to the fine hotel ballroom and even within the portals of the opulent mansions of such powerful families as the Potter Palmers, the Marshall Fields, the Levi Leiters, the McCormicks and the Swifts. All derived their immense fortunes from merchandising, manufacturing, or meat-packing. There was more talk of money in their circles than of blue blood, and a great deal of uninhibited eating, drinking, raucous mirth, boasting, and that vulgarity of manners and display which only the very rich who have risen from nothing by their own thrusting efforts, unrelenting work, and a good deal of ruthlessness, can indulge in without undue regard for the rules of etiquette. The Gold Coast was the name for the district where most such families dwelt and co-mingled, and it was apt.

Pinkerton's Agency served them in many ways, protecting their property, and keeping an eye on the ladies' jewels at the many social functions, and – on a less creditable level – picking up and reporting the gossip and grumbles of the working men and women who provided all the profits, in order that the employers might be forewarned of any labour troubles. Provided we entered the gilded and marbled halls appropriately dressed, and stayed deferential and well behaved, our operatives were treated almost as equals among the guests, which would never have been the case, I gathered, in Boston or New York or Philadelphia.

At one function – I had better not write down the family's name – I became aware that I was the object of the particular attention of an attractive young woman. She was a few years my senior, I learned later; tall and well formed, with an elegant way of carrying herself. Her hair was jet black and she had strikingly dark eyes.

It did not make me feel ill at ease to be stared at by her; it was a fairly general habit, I had found, just as it was the habit of gentlemen, even in these sort of surroundings, to punctuate their conversations about money with plenty of wine and brandy and frequent recourse to the spittoons, which were everywhere.

There was some music going on for dancing. My duty there was to keep a general watch, as a result of rumour picked up by one of our informants that an attempt would be made to steal the jewels which our hostess wore in such profusion that they jingled against each other whenever she moved.

'Spotted your man yet?' a woman's husky low voice asked abruptly, and I found myself looking more closely into the eyes of my persistent scrutineer.

'I beg your pardon, madam?'

'Oh, come. You're the Pinkerton boy. You don't need the Eye embroidered on your shirt front, you know.'

We laughed together.

'No. I've seen no suspicious characters so far. Are there any strangers who strike you as likely candidates?'

'Say, you're English. Don't say Allan's running out of honest Americans.'

I explained why I was spending a few months with his organization.

'I envy you,' she surprised me by saying. 'Do you know, I wanted to join.'

'To join Pinkerton's?'

'Why not? He's employed women detectives before.'

'Have you asked him?' I said.

'Do you honestly see my parents letting me be a detective?'

'I'm afraid I don't know who your parents are, Miss . . .'

'They're your hosts for the evening, that's all,' she said. 'I'm L . . .'

I bowed and introduced myself, with an apology for not having been aware of her identity. I had all along, of course.

escape. She ground her mouth on mine, until I became afraid for my teeth.

I was saved by a sudden commotion from the salon and a woman's scream. My ravisher was paying no attention, and I had to wrestle her away. I stumbled into the room just as a man darted out of the door. The girl was hanging on to me, trying to pull me back, weeping hysterically now. My hair was tousled, my shirt front was crushed, and my stiff collar had come loose.

The hostess stood in the centre of the room, clawing feebly at her throat where several strands of jewelled necklace had been before, but were no longer. She happened to be facing us as we entered, and the girl's weeping caused all other eyes to jerk in our direction.

As the frozen tableau began to move and articulate again, our host stumped towards me and prodded me in the chest with a thick finger that had the impact of an iron bar.

'Call yourself a goddam detective!' he raved. 'Canoodling with that bird-brained minx while the guy you're here to catch gets clean away! For Pete's sake, get after him! Fast!'

For Pete's sake and my own I left the house at great speed. But it was too late; my man had vanished utterly. I should have gone back and searched, in case he was hiding in the house. I chose the discretionary course, and kept going with my back to the place. The Pinkertons were not amused, and I advanced my departure.

The other lady with whom I had a brief passage about this time was of a totally different sort, and came far nearer to disarming me. I met her shortly after my return to London in August 1880. She was the cousin of a casual friend of mine, and I find it hard to write of her, even at this remove.

She was the sweetest, gentlest little woman one could imagine. She was so vulnerable, so defenceless-looking, so grateful for any kindness or courtesy, however small. My friend, thinking to do us both a favour, brought us together, and we went about for quiet, innocent company. I talked about my plans for my agency, and she listened intently, making little remarks and sounds of admiration and encouragement.

She herself had little hobbies; collections of inexpensive items, which she showed me, all neatly arranged, in the apartment where she lived with her kindly aunt, who was always pleased to welcome me. Naturally, if I ever came across an item on a stall which I knew would add to one of the collections I would buy it for her, and her pleasure at receiving it made my heart glow, and she would say something like, 'Oh, thank you so for thinking of me. It makes one feel so . . . so *wanted*, to know that one is thought of, because if one is forgotten, one might not even exist.'

My practice was beginning to develop, and I wanted to start concentrating my mind in earnest, which meant withdrawing into the almost monastic way of life which was an important feature of my plan. I managed to spend less time with my friend, explaining how busy I was becoming and how much I needed to concentrate. She gave me little wistful smiles, and lowered her eyes, and said that of course she understood; and her aunt looked sad and said how they missed my visits.

To cast her off would be tantamount to abandoning a puppy dog. Worse, because she would say some bright, brave little thing about understanding perfectly, and would show me some small piece which she had managed to find for one of the collections, implying that at least she would have something left to fill the void.

I took the cowardly way, and simply did not call on her again. I knew that she would never be so forward as to come calling on me.

I read, years later, that she had been hanged for poisoning three little children for their insurance-money. Be that as it may, she was quite the most winning woman I ever knew.

No, I am not the marrying type of man. I cannot take without giving in return, and I am afraid I have had nothing to offer a wife. I should have been a disappointment, and filled her with remorse at her failure to do anything with me, which, of course, she would have blamed upon herself.

As to children – again, alas. I picture myself seated on my pile of cushions, deeply immersed in a three-pipe problem, and from the next room arises the clamour of infants disputing their bedtime. Great heavens, some poor innocent fellow's life might have been forfeited on the gallows through such interruption of my thought processes!

Irene Adler? Ah, she was *the* woman; but it was not I who had to take on the responsibility of marrying her, or I fear my admiration for her might have become much modified by now.

STREET OF MEMORIES

I DESCRIBED this present (and, I trust, last) abode of mine in the account of the case of *The Lion's Mane*, which I was compelled to write myself, the good Watson having by that time (1907) passed almost beyond my ken. I had been retired four years, and it has puzzled some of those who profess interest in my career why and how a man of my restless and inquiring disposition could have given up his work at the early age of forty-nine to bury himself in the isolation of a remote corner of Sussex.

The decision to retire was not a difficult one. If Watson is anyone to go by, I was already past my peak, which he reckoned to have been attained in 1895. I say *if* he is anyone to go by, of which I am not at all certain. With his tendencies to romanticism and his fatal habit of looking at everything from the point of view of a drama instead of as a scientific exercise he was far from ideally equipped to judge my investigations on their true merits. From many which took place in that busy year he chose to narrate five: in his nomenclature, they are *The Three Students, The Solitary Cyclist, Black Peter, The Norwood Builder* and *The Bruce-Partington Plans*. Somewhat typically of him he employs the term 'famous' of my inquiry carried out that year at the express wish of His Holiness the Pope into the sudden death of Cardinal Tosca, yet does not go on to give its details; and, to my mind at least, he deprived his public of a chronicle of great potential interest and much scope for sensation by merely mentioning in passing my arrest of Wilson, the notorious canary-trainer, which removed a plague-spot from the East End of London.

Perhaps there were features of my handling of those cases of which Watson personally disapproved. He had many quirks and quite prim prejudices for a self-professed man of the world. But even excluding them, I accept, with some reservations, his contention that '95 had been my vintage year. The Bruce-Partington submarine matter did earn me my summons to Windsor Castle to receive gracious thanks and the gift of the emerald tie-pin which my dislike of ostentatious display has kept shut away in its little box all these years. Even so, on re-reading his narrative, I find I am right in remembering that by the end of the year I was complaining that the London criminal as a species had become a dull fellow, who in better days would have taken more advantage of the dense yellow fogs which blanketed the metropolis late that November.

It cannot be surprising that Watson should have seen me in better mental form than ever in that year. I had risen from the dead only the year before (oh dear! I shall somehow have to

Threadneedle Street, with the Bank of England on the right. The City's second largest private bank, Holder & Stevenson, at the centre of THE BERYL CORONET *case was also in this street, and the crippled beggar, Hugh Boone, whom I unmasked in* THE MAN WITH THE TWISTED LIP, *had his regular pitch near this spot.*

tackle that business if I am to keep this memoir going). After three years away from my profession I was buoyant and eager to get back to work, while the underworld, which had fallen into incautious ways since my supposed death, had left more than the usual number of loose ends lying about for me to pick up where the official police had missed them.

Someone during those last years of the century remarked, however, that although I had come back I was never again quite the same as I had been before. I dare say there was truth in that. Part of my function had been taken over by the police, through their advances in forensic science and their improved efficiency and morale since the militancy of 1890 which had brought their grievances to a head. I continued with my practice, though, until Watson took unto himself his second wife in 1902, leaving me alone in Baker Street again. It seemed time to go, to give myself up to that soothing life of Nature for which I had so often yearned during a quarter of a century spent amid the gloom of London.

Apart from the Lion's Mane business and another semi-local matter, though of wider import, subsequently chronicled as *His Last Bow*, I have been inactive ever since. (I do not allude to a couple of cases which I must exclude even from these private notes because of their international nature.)

Yet what is inactivity? I have kept my bees. I have added to my *oeuvre* of monographs on a number of subjects. Admittedly, I have never written that definitive textbook of the art of detection which I envisaged to Watson during our investigation at the Abbey Grange, in Kent. I am out of date now. With their laboratories, fingerprints, photography, training school for detectives and all the rest of it the police have outstripped me. The modern equivalent of the Lestrades and Gregsons are a different breed from the CID intake of '78 who replaced those broken in the so-called Trial of the Detectives in the year before. The day of the lone freelance is over, and I have no longer any guidance to offer. I did not write that book; but in more than a thousand cases successfully pursued I have written my Book of Life, and much of my time has been spent in mentally reviewing its contents.

Nothing has developed to change my contention that the cultivated and ceaselessly practised powers of observation and deduction, backed up with a wide range of exact knowledge from which to draw precedents and explanations, are the qualities still essential in the detective, even in an age when science and the use of informants within the criminal ranks have to a great extent superseded ratiocination. Had I written my treatise, I should have illustrated it with instances of these and other facets of my own methods.

In speaking of observation, I should have drawn attention to such cases as *A Scandal in Bohemia, A Study in Scarlet* and *A Case of Identity*. Of deduction, I should have quoted my axiom that the more *outré* and grotesque an incident is, the more carefully it deserves to be examined. There would have followed an example of my habit of first studying the scene and objects associated with a crime and gathering all available evidence, first-hand and reported, and then withdrawing with my hoard into what Watson termed, in relating the case of *The Hound of the Baskervilles*, 'those hours of intense mental concentration during which he weighed every particle of evidence, constructed alternative theories, balanced one against the other, and made up his mind as to which points were essential and which immaterial.' In essence, my favourite maxim remains: 'When you have excluded the impossible, whatever remains, however improbable, must be the truth.'

As to knowledge, I hold it more important to know where to find facts in precise form than to attempt to retain them all in one's brain, where they can become jumbled, distorted, over-laid and even submerged without trace. As I put it in my account of *The Lion's Mane*: 'My mind is like a crowded box-room with packets of all sorts stowed away therein – so many that I may well have but a vague perception of what was there.'

Watson, in *A Study in Scarlet*, lists the limits of my know-ledge of various subjects and finds the results amusing and deplorable. But he came nearer to understanding my principle when he quoted that other remark of mine: 'A man should keep his little brain attic stocked with all the furniture that he is likely to use, and the rest he can put away in the lumber-room of his library, where he can get it if he wants it.' I hold that even the wonderful human brain has its limits, and that there is a danger that in trying to cram extra into the memory, something of equal value might get squeezed out.

My repository for much of what I wished to store has always been my commonplace books, which I still keep up to date, a

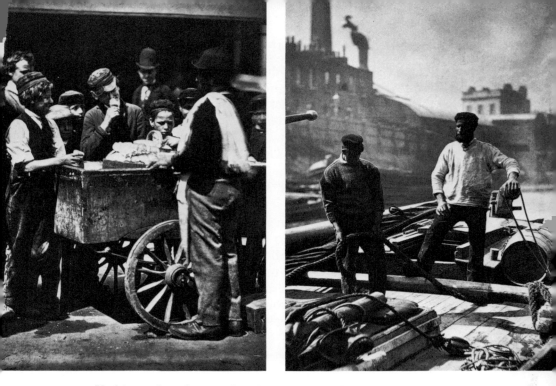

LEFT: *Urchins such as these, gathered at a street-vendor's cart, were the type of 'street Arab' who constituted my Baker Street Irregulars. In such cases as* A STUDY IN SCARLET, THE SIGN OF FOUR *and* THE CROOKED MAN *their ability to go anywhere unremarked proved invaluable, at a shilling a day each.*

RIGHT: *Thames bargees, whose language was noted for its violence and idiomatic range. Many of my investigations took me onto the foul-smelling river and its sinister hinterland, and it was the scene of our great boat chase after the Agra treasure in* THE SIGN OF FOUR *in September 1888.*

labour which accounts for many absorbed hours each day. I do not think that Watson ever believed my contention that I read nothing in the daily newspapers save the criminal news and the agony column, but those were the sections from which I culled most of what fills these albums of mine. I may have termed the agony column a chorus of groans, cries and bleatings; but I was not exaggerating when I added that they provided the most valuable hunting-ground that ever was given to a student of the unusual, and the only open means of intercepting messages intended for persons who prefer not to be reached by letter or other direct means.

It was in the agony column of *The Times* that I noticed the Countess of Morcar's advertisement for her missing precious stone, and so was able to identify it when Commissionaire Peterson brought it to me and set in motion the case of *The Blue Carbuncle*. I used the *Standard*'s agony column to advertise for Mordecai Smith's steam launch *Aurora* in investigating *The Sign of Four*; and that poor deluded Mary Sutherland advertised in the *Chronicle* for her errant gas-fitter in *A Case of Identity*. Oh yes, the Press is a most valuable institution if you only know how to use it. I demonstrated that in tracking down *The Six Napoleons*.

My other invaluable source of information was dear old Watson. When I remarked to him during the *Sussex Vampire* business, 'I never get your limits, Watson; there are unexplored possibilities about you,' I was not being sardonic. He really was a mine of information, as much from what he did not understand or perceive as from what he did. In that narrative which he challenged me to write myself, *The Blanched Soldier*, I stated: 'I would take this opportunity to remark that if I burden myself with a companion in my various little inquiries it is not done out of sentiment or caprice, but it is that Watson has some remarkable characteristics of his own to which in his modesty he has given small attention amid his exaggerated estimates of my own performances. A confederate to whom each new development comes as a perpetual surprise, and to whom the future is always a closed book, is an ideal helpmate.'

His special subjects were the turf and women, and since my investigations featured both at one time or another I was able to draw upon his advice, though not wholly to trust it, for he was highly susceptible on both accounts and therefore incapable of pure objectivity.

Once the initial economic necessity had passed, which it did quite quickly under the influence of my swift success at my occupation, there was no necessity to keep Watson on at Baker Street. I should not have dreamed of asking him to move out, though, and he only did so in order to keep getting married. Even then I was often round to his house to seek his companionship in some adventure. He never refused me. He was a brave and loyal companion in any danger, and although he would sulk a little and look hurt when I ribbed him or made unexplained use of him, as for instance in *The Hound of the Baskervilles*, and even thrust him into danger without fore-warning in *The Speckled Band* and *The Illustrious Client*, he always forgave me when all was accomplished and explained. Shocking him with my 'death' and leaving him to mourn me for three years would have been inhumane, had it been avoidable (I shall *have* to write it all down yet; I can see it coming!).

I expect there will be those who will wonder how a man of my solitary preferences and admittedly selfish proclivities could have borne to share my quarters with another person, particularly one whose everyday habits were so different from mine. When we were not working together, and I filled in the time with my intellectual pursuits, he would go off to play billiards at Thurston's in Leicester Square, visit his clubs, place his bets, drink with his theatrical cronies, watch them act, squire women about town, sit interminably at Lord's cricket ground; some clue generally told me which it had been, if I was not too preoccupied to notice his return. He ate heavy meals at every opportunity and made hearty remarks to Mrs Hudson and Billy, her occasional pageboy. If I was unoccupied, and therefore bored, it irritated me sometimes to the point of making some sarcastic jibe, which I regretted later. But if my mind was concentrated on a problem, I could shut myself off from him mentally, retreating into my cocoon of loneliness and isolation which none could penetrate. He quickly learned to gauge my accessibility, as did Mrs Hudson, and to accept that I would use them and make myself available to them only as and when it suited me. In this manner he and I got on as well as two friendly brothers, of wholly differing natures but with firm mutual understanding and respect.

In every domestic and professional regard it was infinitely preferable to a marriage. A wife would have made demands on me. She would have fussed me, and tidied my papers, and refused to have my correspondence impaled to the mantelpiece with a jack-knife and my cigars occupying the coal scuttle. That occasion when I was investigating the loss of the Mazarin Stone and told Mrs Hudson that I should be back to dine at 'seven-thirty, the day after tomorrow' would have produced from any Mrs Holmes the stern riposte, 'Sherlock, I particularly require you back *this* evening at seven; the Watsons are coming in for a hand of whist.'

Once, in one of Watson's married phases, I unwarily accepted his invitation to dine at his home. His wife of the time was the former Mary Morstan, a girl of sweetness and charac-

My skill at disguise enabled me to penetrate unmolested the worst slum areas of the East End and Dockland, where uniformed police ventured only in numbers. These poor people, whose plight moved me deeply, posed for me as an itinerant photographer.

ter whom he had met when she came to me with the problem of *The Sign of Four*, but observing Watson playing husband to her was like watching a Samson creeping about with his hair shorn.

Mrs Hudson knew precisely where to draw the line. She lived unobtrusively in her rooms at the foot of the house and in her basement kitchen. We were vaguely aware of the comings and goings of cronies of hers, but they never set foot on our stairs. She possessed an anticipation of our needs which bordered on the uncanny – something to do with her Scottish second sight, no doubt. Although Watson was a predictably regular consumer of food and drink, my own habits were erratic as to timing and requirements, yet she seemed able to divine both. One had but to touch the bell and there would shortly follow her stately tread up to our door. She would enter bearing coffee, luncheon, tea and muffins, dinner, or our boots, exactly as the moment required, without any orders having been given. The numerous editions of all the newspapers and the twelve deliveries of post which came day and evening were brought in as soon as they arrived, as also were clients of mine by appointment.

The more welcome, if I were in desultory mood, would be Mrs Hudson announcing some stranger in distress, come to seek an interview but fully expecting to be turned away, not ushered into the basket chair and handed a glass of Watson's prescription for any ill or fear, brandy and soda.

The only visitors the good lady could not abide were those ragged urchins whom I dubbed the Baker Street Irregulars, who, being what they were and looking as they did, could go everywhere, see everything and overhear everyone without being suspected as my agents. Mrs Hudson would have forbidden them her premises if she had dared. I made only infrequent use of them, but they amply proved their value by their assistance in the cases of *A Study in Scarlet, The Sign of Four* and *The Crooked Man.*

I should have liked it if Mrs Hudson had accompanied me here when I retired, but I did not even ask it of her. The country quiet would not have suited her. She would have missed the Baker Street traffic, the constant tramp of feet past her house, the shadows passing her area window, the shouts, the hooves and wheels, the palpitation of mighty London. Martha fills her place well enough with her twice-daily visits. She has not Mrs Hudson's finely-tuned respect for my brand of untidiness; and if I were to get out my revolver and shoot the initials G.R. in the wall, assuming my aim to be still steady enough, I am sure I should never see her again.

I can still see the V.R. in the Baker Street wall, though I have not set foot in the rooms since leaving them in 1903 to come here. I wonder whether Mrs Hudson, or her successor,

has had them plastered over? I doubt that she herself ever would. Watson's report, apropos that time I pretended to be dying so as to trap one of my would-be murderers, was that she was fond of me as well as awed. Our respect, too, was mutual.

The bullet-pocked V.R., the jack-knife transfixing the unanswered correspondence, the cigars in the coal scuttle, the tobacco in the old Persian slipper in the hearth, the wax bust with the bullet hole through its head, the poker bent double by the fuming Dr Grimesby Roylott and straightened again by my own hands, the walking sticks, the harpoon, the pipes, the chemical apparatus – I can visualize them all still in their places in that sanctum of ours. Some of them are about me here, but no detail escapes me of them in that long-familiar setting of those now rapidly receding days when Watson and I sat in our respective armchairs at either side of the fire, our post-breakfast pipes aglow and a crumpled pile of newspapers growing about our ankles, awaiting the first sound of my expected client's foot upon the stair. Those were the halcyon days of alternating high adventure and slippered ease. It would have been a mistake to try to perpetuate them with my occupation virtually gone, and Watson gone too. A clean break was required, and none could have been cleaner, metaphorically and literally, than coming here.

The 'chestiness' (as they term in my native North country any form of respiratory weakness) which had troubled me in boyhood had left its legacy. Had a regard for my health been uppermost I should have recoiled from London as the place in which to pass the best years of my life. Those rolling yellow fogs with which Watson has heightened the atmosphere of his tales killed hundreds of people annually with their all-permeating acid fumes. They stifled and choked, confused groping wayfarers into blundering under horses' hooves or breaking their necks falling down into areas whose gates had been left thoughtlessly open. They provided cover for the foot-pad and the thug to strike his blow, snatch his loot, and vanish. As I remarked to Watson shortly before we were precipitated

The underfed flower girls outside Covent Garden market made a pitiful contrast with the well-groomed patrons of the Royal Opera House whose pennies they sought. The market itself featured prominently in one of my most enjoyable cases, THE BLUE CARBUNCLE, *during the Festive Season of 1887.*

Piccadilly Circus, a view taken after the unveiling of Sir
Alfred Gilbert's 'Eros' (left) in 1893. Behind Eros stands
the Criterion, where Watson's meeting with his old colleague
Stamford in the American Bar on New Year's Day 1881 resulted
in his introduction to me, recounted in A STUDY IN SCARLET.

into the Bruce-Partington case, in which that fog of November 1895 played its part, 'It is well they don't have days of fog in the Latin countries – the countries of assassination.'

There was nothing the least romantic about a pea-souper; and even when there was no fog at all there hung over all London an almost perpetual cloud of brownish yellow soot from the factory chimneys and household fires of cheap coal which burnt the year round as the only means of cooking food or heating water in even the hottest weather.

This stationary cloud which dirtied the clothes on one's back, begrimed the laundry hung out to dry and caked one's lungs was but a reflection of the filth below: the mud or dust which covered every surface of road and pavement, attached itself to shoes and spats, trouser bottoms and the trailing hems of women's dresses. Its stink was ever-present, added to by the pungent reek of the droppings of the tens of thousands of horses which filled the streets in unregulated confusion. The odour from the sewers and from that vast open drain, the River Thames, pervaded everywhere; while day and night there persisted that other form of nuisance, noise, from the shouting and cursing of the innumerable horse-drivers in their terrible traffic jams and the counter-abuse of pedestrians risking their lives to cross the roads; the shrilling of newsboys, the jangling and braying of the instruments of wandering musicians, the rough chants of street vendors, the clash of hooves and clanking and creaking of every sort of vehicle, cabs, carts, carriages, horse-drawn omnibuses and their earliest motor equivalents.

London was filthy, smelly, noisy and extremely dangerous, not only to the health and sanity of the populace and the many risks to their limbs in going about their most innocent pursuits – the casualty wards of the many hospitals were always packed with victims of accidents – but from the high level of vicious-ness and crime, which amounted to about one-third of all that perpetrated throughout the country.

In a city devoid of crime, of course, I should have been with-out an occupation; but the scope of my investigations did not include the commonplace. The problems which my clients laid before me, or in which the police condescended to seek my help, tended to the abstruse and the bizarre, outside the con-ventions of humdrum routine and often beyond the confines of London itself. I chose only to be associated with crimes which presented some difficulty in their solution, some testing of those skills which I had acquired, those theories which I had formulated, those precedents which experience had shown me. My clientèle came from all ranks and walks of life; and, contrary to Watson's report, my fees varied considerably, according to means, but were sometimes remitted altogether.

I have been asked many times which of them represented my greatest 'triumphs'. It is hard to be objective. I fancy that in terms of sheer application of my principles of detection I was never better than in *The Naval Treaty* and *The Valley of Fear*, while observation and cunning deception, as much as the culprit's recklessness, brought me success in *The Hound of the Baskervilles*. A keen awareness of human cupidity was in-valuable in the case of *The Blue Carbuncle*, while all that the daily newspapers had taught me of that enduring gullibility which has enabled the confidence trickster to flourish down the ages led me to the solution of that extraordinary ruse, *The Red-Headed League*. My skill at disguise was given a thorough testing in *A Scandal in Bohemia*, failing only to deceive Miss Irene Adler, whom I have since admired above all women for her combination of femininity and acumen.

So far as high drama goes, *The Speckled Band* remains most vivid in my memory, although honesty would force me to ascribe my success to intuition rather than logical deduction. It seemed full of promise, as related to me by the bereaved Miss Stoner: the orphaned twin heiresses in the guardianship of the violent stepfather, Dr Roylott; the ruined family estate, on which a cheetah and a baboon wandered freely and gipsies camped; some exchanging of bedrooms due to repair work; a whistle and metallic clang in the night, followed by the death of Julia Stoner, gasping out the last words, 'It was the band! The speckled band!'

As Watson has told the world, I deduced a deadly snake, passed through a ventilator to slither down the dummy bell rope to reach its victim, and recalled after doing its work by Dr Roylott's whistle, when it was rewarded with its saucer of milk and locked away in the metal safe where it unaccountably lived without becoming suffocated. Even at this remove in time, I am forced to blush at the glib offhandedness with which I explained it all. Snakes are deaf and do not drink milk. To admit the simple truth, I guessed, rather than deduced, and fortunately correctly. 'I had come to an entirely erroneous conclusion,' I admitted to Watson as we made our way homeward in the train. (I was referring only to my supposition that the gipsies had been involved.) Having let him sit there in the dark, all unsuspecting of the snake's approach, I had not the heart to tell him how much of my confidence had been based on guesswork. Remembering it now, down the years, I seem to hear that once-familiar voice of Professor Moriarty chiding, 'Dear me, Mr Holmes, dear me!'

So much for random recollection. Instinct tells me that I have now reached my Rubicon and must decide whether to cross. Should I do so, it will entail telling that which I suppose I am under perpetual oath never to reveal. The question is, in writing for my eyes alone, am I revealing anything at all? I must put aside my pen and pad, and apply my old mind to that nowadays unaccustomed exercise, a three-pipe problem.

A Summons to the
Diogenes Club

WHEN I commenced this retrospective journey of the mind, using Watson's chronicles for my *Baedeker*, I envisaged my progress as nothing more than an aimless amble along random tracks, some familiar, others forgotten. The last thing I had foreseen was coming upon an obstacle at which I should have to halt, and perhaps turn back.

That is what has happened to me now, and deciding what to do about it cost me several extra pipes last night, with a consequent accompaniment of whisky; Martha's glance at me this morning, followed by her frown at the decanter, told its own story. She sniffed her distaste for the atmosphere, and although it is quite nippy for early autumn, flung open all the sitting-room windows.

As I reminded myself repeatedly, these jottings were intended as mere footnotes to my story as Watson has represented it. I am under no compulsion to go further; and yet, it occurred to me somewhere about the deep of last midnight, perhaps it is nothing less than my duty to record what really did happen at the Reichenbach Falls on that afternoon in May 1891, when Professor James Moriarty and I engaged in what the world has always supposed to have been a fatal struggle.

The particulars of what did happen, and how it came about, and what followed, do exist. They occupy what I am sure are bulky and sealed files somewhere in Whitehall's dustier depths, consigned there by my brother Mycroft with his own HIGHLY SECRET and STRICTLY CONFIDENTIAL labels. There they will no doubt lie until some period has elapsed after which it may be considered feasible to permit historians access to them without fear of international embarrassment and repercussions. From what I have experienced of Whitehall and its ways, as exemplified by my devious brother, when that time comes, and some scholar makes his application to examine the documents, they will be found to have been 'mislaid' or even 'disappeared'. There will be a brief furore in the press – perhaps as much as a question in the House, blandly turned aside – and that will be the end of the affair. The only remaining version will be that which Watson recorded, at my instigation – and which, all unknown to that most honest of beings, was a sheer pack of lies.

There stands my barrier, my obstacle. Am I to shy from it, and creep away; or is it my responsibility, nay, bounden duty, to set down the true particulars as I alone know them?

Such was the question I asked myself in this morning's earliest hours, and, a pipe or two later, answered in the affirmative. This work was not embarked on with any view to publication. When I am gone, though, it will be found, and subjected to study by some of the more diligent of those people who have evinced keen interest in the minutiae of my career. I shall be beyond caring what they make of it, and the government of the day will have no difficulty in dissociating itself from events of long ago, with the Official Secrets Acts of 1911 and 1920 to invoke as its safeguard.

Here goes, then. I will expend some care on what follows, in the consciousness that, in a small way, I shall be found to have been rewriting history.

The story goes back to an April evening – Thursday, the 23rd, in that 'fateful' year of 1891. I had returned at about eleven o'clock to 221B Baker Street, my solitary abode since Watson's marriage in 1889 and removal to Paddington. I was in evening attire, having come from a dinner given in my honour by a leading firm of bankers to whom I had been of some service. It had been a discreet occasion, so much so that I had not told Mrs Hudson where I was going, or how long I might be absent.

Consequently, my return found her pacing agitatedly in the downstairs lobby. She hurried to me with every show of relief.

'Why, Mrs Hudson, what is the matter? Is the Prime Minister waiting upstairs?'

'Worse than that, sir,' the good lady replied. 'A message from Mr Mycroft Holmes.'

'He will be flattered when I tell him of your comparison – although, come to think of it, it is no doubt in keeping with his estimate of himself.'

'Beg pardon, Mr Holmes?'

'Never mind. What is his message, pray?'

'Ye're to go to that Dioginnus Club, sir.'

'The Diogenes. In the morning?'

'No, sir. Tonight.'

'At what time did the message come?'

'An hour since, sir. Och, I've been a' agley, wondering when ye'd get back.'

'Dinnae fash yersel,' I answered, in my approximation to her Scottish accent. My hosts had plied me with several excellent wines and superb port and brandy.

'Beg pardon, sir?'

I sighed. 'Don't worry. It is well past my brother's hour. He will have gone home to bed long since. I'll step along tomorrow, at his usual time.'

'Noo, noo, sir. You're to go there without fail or delay. "Fail or delay" was the words.'

'Whose words?'

'An old man in a uniform coat. He had a cab waiting. Very dour sort of way with him, I thought.'

'The Diogenes manner. Ah, me. It is a sure sign that he will be waiting there for me.'

Resuming my hat and cane, I went out once more into the night. Fortunately, it was fine. One thing was certain: no porter at the Diogenes Club would have demeaned himself to carry a message unless it had been at the command of one of the few founder members, of whom my brother was one. The staff's taciturnity and unhelpfulness was legendary, and therefore much appreciated by the members of that club for unclubbable men in Pall Mall. Mycroft knew as well as I did that my premises were often watched by agents of the Moriarty gang and other anti-social combinations. Any of them strolling out of the shadows to ask a Diogenes Club employee for a light, and trying to strike up conversation in the hope of gleaning information, would have got neither.

It followed, therefore, that Mycroft's summons was as mandatory and important as Mrs Hudson had conveyed. His club hours were an almost unvarying quarter to five till twenty past eight, but it was now gone eleven. I took the precaution of walking some way down Baker Street before doubling back through some alleyways and hailing a cab, in case any curious follower had attached himself to me.

The Diogenes was a fittingly morose edifice of stone construction, excessively pillared and balustraded in that otherwise elegant street of clubs, Pall Mall. Its chief rule was that no member was permitted to take the least notice of any other, from which it logically followed that there was no talking allowed, save in the Strangers' Room. It was not there, however, that, having been denied the pleasure of finding me to be some ignoramus who had mistaken the premises for the Athenaeum or the Reform and shutting the door in my face, the porter led me without a word past the glass-panelled rooms in which the few members present were feeding their misanthropy from the early editions of next day's newspapers, to a door marked COMMITTEE. He knocked thrice. I heard a key turned, and the door opened a fraction, to show me my brother's saurian eye.

'About time, Sherlock,' he murmured, having silently gesticulated to the attendant to leave us. 'Come in.'

I noticed that, before admitting me, he opened the door just sufficiently to crane his thick neck round it and peer both ways along the passage, satisfying himself that no one else was about. He ushered me in quickly and hastily turned the key in the inside lock.

For all their establishment's reputation, it was clear that the Diogenes Club's committee believed in doing itself proudly. Their sanctum was long and narrow, its walls and low ceiling faced with dark oak panelling, either transferred from older interiors or reproduced from Tudor originals to create an appropriately sombre effect. A long, gleaming walnut table stretched to the distant windows, where tapestried curtains were close drawn.

Glasses and decanters glistened at that end of the table, which lay in the subdued light of candles in black iron holders: no gas lamps were in evidence. Indeed, at first glance I was not aware of any other human presence; but as I stepped away from the door in my brother's bulky wake I perceived a movement, and saw a figure slowly uncoil itself from one of the shadowed dining chairs in the distance.

Pall Mall, the street containing some of London's most notable gentlemen's clubs. Idiosyncratic would be a better description of the Diogenes Club, my brother Mycroft's home-from-home near this spot. Its members comprised the capital's most unsociable and unclubbable men, who ignored one another assiduously.

The hall of a London club – NOT *the Diogenes, where such evidence of service would be absent! At the Diogenes I had the momentous meeting with Professor Moriarty which was the prelude to the bizarre adventure set down in these pages for the first time.*

There would have been no mistaking him in a brightly-lit crowd of ten thousand: the great height and cadaverous frame, with shoulders rounded from much study; the curved white dome of forehead, rendered even more skull-like by the deeply sunken eyes; and, most tell-tale of all, the reptilian oscillation from side to side of the pale, unsmiling face, which regarded me with peering, puckered eyes.

As I later told Watson in my spurious account of this meeting, which I led him to believe had taken place at Baker Street, 'My nerves are fairly proof, but I confess to a start when I saw the very man who had been so much in my thoughts standing there.' I had not seen him previously, but his identity was beyond doubt, and Mycroft's introduction wholly superfluous: 'Mr Sherlock Holmes – Professor James Moriarty.'

MEETING MORIARTY

He came slowly round the length of the table to stand before me. That hypnotic oscillation of his head never ceased, yet his eyes remained fixed on mine, as if seeking to probe into my very thoughts. His hands were behind his back. He did not withdraw one to offer in greeting. For my own part I made no move. He studied my forehead keenly.

'You have less frontal development than I should have expected,' he said at last. His voice was cultivated and slow, with protracted sibilants which added to the impression of a reptile. 'All the same, you are succeeding in proving a nuisance to me, Mr Sherlock Holmes.'

'It is my business to prove a nuisance to such as yourself, Professor,' was my reply.

'You mean, you make it your business. You delight in taking it upon yourself to do so.'

The cold eyes had flickered momentarily with a flash of anger. I saw that a much deeper resentment lay beneath, controlled with difficulty, and I felt sudden alarm that he might suspect that my long campaign to topple his empire of crime was nearing its culmination. There had been a more than customary number of attempts to kill or disable me of late. Knowing the man and his methods, it occurred to me that, having failed in that line, he had found it necessary to approach my brother, the *éminence grise* of Whitehall, with some proposal – for instance, Mycroft, with his wide-ranging discretionary powers, would call me off his track, Moriarty would spare the government, or perhaps one of its erring Ministers, some public disclosure which carried the certainty of damaging repercussions.

I knew my brother. He owed his clandestine status within the corridors of power to an abnormally acute brain, allied to a cunning which Machiavelli himself would have admired.

He would have gained high office or lost his head (no doubt both) at one of those medieval courts which I had often thought would have been his ideal sphere. It was not in him to march into the Foreign Office or No. 10 Downing Street and report a blackmailer's approach, counselling measures which would enable him to return to buy off the blackmailer, or tell him to publish and be damned.

No; Mycroft, that playmate of my childhood who, when facing defeat in some innocent game, would suddenly 'remember' some rule of which I had never heard, which would undermine my position and advantage, would turn to no one else for help in a crisis. That would be too much like admitting his own weakness, compromising the structure of power which he had spent years in building from the comfort of sundry armchairs in his offices and club, and the bachelor apartments which lay within short walking distance of them all.

'Gentlemen, gentlemen!' he admonished, puffing his corpulent way towards us with glasses of brandy for each. In my intent scrutiny of the supreme enemy with whom I had been brought face to face at last, I had not noticed Mycroft leave our side, but his ears had not failed to note the edge to our exchange while he had been occupied with the decanter.

'Pray don't acidulate your palates against Hennessy '40 with such bitter tones. Why, with the mutual admiration you entertain, I should have thought this meeting might be regarded as memorable.'

'Oh, indeed,' said Moriarty, and sniffed deeply into his glass. 'Most memorable. Tut-tut, though. I confess disappointment at such lack of frontal development. It goes far to support my belief that your brother's success has owed more to chance than to that capacity of brain with which I had always credited him.' He studied the brandy carefully.

'That will *do*, Professor, if you please!' snapped Mycroft, whose languid manner was capable of quite sudden change. 'Let us observe the civilities.'

'Civilities!' it was my turn to protest. 'You do realize, Mycroft, that this fiend from whom you believe my sensibilities need defending is the organizer of half that is evil and nearly all that is undetected in this great city.'

'A genius, though, you must concede,' Moriarty insisted with a little smile.

'Only in the sense that the spider is the genius of his web. He does little, save sit motionless at its centre, and spin. The web does his work for him after that.'

'Ah, but it is the ability to spin that web – to choose its most effective location – to interpret every quiver of each of its thousand radiations.'

'That is craftsmanship, not genius,' I retorted. 'It is inherent in the nature of all spiders to spin webs and interpret their vibrations. Genius is a limited preserve . . .'

'Splendid, splendid!' Mycroft broke in. 'You are getting along famously already. Every instinct told me that you would stimulate one another. That is where *my* genius lies.'

Moriarty and I turned as one, to stare at him.

'"Getting along"?' echoed the Professor. '"Stimulate"? What in heaven's name is that supposed to mean?'

'Do sit down, Professor. Then perhaps my brother will follow suit. We shall have him prowling about, otherwise, which is unsettling to the nerves.'

'If you are so concerned for your nerves these days,' I told him, 'you should know better than to send for me to bandy words in front of you with a man who has tried to have me killed three times in the last two days.'

Moriarty sank into one of the dining chairs, placed his glass on the table, and raised his hands in a gesture of despair.

'You are not, by any chance, referring to that runaway horse van? Dear me, Mr Holmes, was that you? The incident was quite the talk of Marylebone High Street that afternoon. They say the driver was dreadfully shaken by the time he regained control.'

'Not as "shaken" as he had been instructed to leave me, if a policeman's shout hadn't warned me. I suppose you also happened to hear of the falling brick which just missed my head in Vere Street that same afternoon?'

'You don't say! From that house undergoing roof repairs, I'll wager. It is a positive scandal that they should leave bricks and tiles piled so high above a busy pavement.'

'Scandalous – but convenient for a mathematical coach who was, I dare say, demonstrating problems on a blackboard for one of his pupils miles away, having deputed his evil purpose to some minion, who knows he will be disowned and left to take the punishment if he is caught in the act.'

'I think, gentlemen. . . .' Mycroft tried to interrupt, but my irritation was by now almost beyond bounds.

'Just in case you are wondering what has become of your rough who tried to take me with a bludgeon in Paddington earlier today, he is in police custody.' I brandished a grazed right fist at Moriarty across the table. 'You owe him a set of dentures, in lieu of the teeth I knocked out of his head. But I can tell you,' I turned to Mycroft, 'that no possible connection will ever be traced between him and this "gentleman".'

Moriarty tut-tutted deprecatingly, and examined his nails. It was my brother's turn to take up the talking.

'Now that you two have had the chance, and taken every opportunity, to sniff around one another like two dogs on first acquaintance (if you will forgive any crudity in the metaphor), I will invite your attention. I wish to tell you why I have summoned you here, and will ask you kindly not to interrupt until I have done. Sherlock, just be so good as to fetch the brandy up the table, so as to avoid interruption later.'

Moriarty began his uncoiling process. 'I think it is about time I took my leave, he murmured. 'I anticipate a busy day, with an early start. . . .'

'Kindly remain seated, Professor,' Mycroft said, and his tone was not that of a request. 'And, Sherlock, we will dispense with gibes from now onward. There are matters of no small seriousness to discuss.'

I was about to retort that attempts on my life were of some seriousness to me, but forbore, and resumed my seat across the table from Moriarty, with Mycroft between us at its foot. He turned first to address Moriarty, who had allowed his skull-like dome to sink forward into a waiting attitude, yet still keeping up that slight to and fro motion which seemed to add to the depth of his concentration on my brother's words.

'In a very short time, Professor Moriarty, your organization will be smashed.'

'Mycroft . . .' I interrupted sharply, anxious to forestall any disclosure which might coincidentally give away my plans for that blow to be struck.

'*Please*, Sherlock, *no* interruptions,' Mycroft insisted, and his usually benign, jowly countenance seemed transformed to that hardness which I had only seen it assume at times of grave juncture.

'The three of us in this room are the only people beside certain high police officers who know that on Monday the organization which Professor Moriarty has spent many years creating, and which has served society so ill, will be finished.'

A silence hung. Monday was my day, the day for which a great police operation was poised, its objectives defined, its men instructed, yet none of them knowing that his individual assignment was but a part of a gigantic coup which would result in the greatest mass criminal round-up of the century and, as I confidently expected, the clearing up of over forty mysteries.

Monday – and I had just heard my brother, the most influential man behind the Whitehall scenes, name it to the spider-figure who had spun the web which on that day was to be ripped to shreds, and the spider himself torn from its centre. For a moment no one spoke. Then:

'This is a unique occasion, gentlemen,' continued Mycroft, breaking our mutual silence. 'An historic one. I myself am conscious of the privilege of sharing in it; indeed, of having brought it about. I seek, and shall get, no credit; and from the way you are each regarding me I fear I can anticipate little in the way of personal thanks.'

'For my part,' Moriarty put in, 'the only thanks likely to be forthcoming will be if you will come quickly to the point.'

'Professor, you have heard me rebuke my brother for interrupting. Now it is your turn.'

'Your brother may act the lackey to you, if he chooses – though I fancy you will not enjoy his services for much longer. I accept orders from no one.'

'Save the Devil,' I was unable to prevent myself interpolating. 'Though I don't doubt there are times when he does as you tell him.'

'Be *quiet,* Sherlock!'

'Oh, don't be sharp with your young brother, Mr Holmes. I can defend myself against his puny barbs. But I really think that if we are to allow metaphysics to enter these deliberations, we are in danger of remaining here all night.'

'I quite agree, Professor,' nodded Mycroft. 'To a man of science such as yourself, all talk of metaphysics – religion, even – must be particularly irrelevant.'

'That is so.'

'I am glad to have the point clear from your own lips. In short, science holds the key to all problems? Its service and advancement justify any means?'

'Anything under the sun.'

'Tell me, Professor – is your devotion to a career of (pardon the expression) crime a part of your desire to advance the cause of science?'

'I confess to no crimes.'

I beat the table top. 'He only plans them, for others to carry out. If his agent is caught, money appears from thin air to pay for his bail or his defence. Moriarty himself never enters into it – is never even suspected.'

'Yes, yes,' said Mycroft, without troubling to rebuke me further, and speaking so matter-of-factly that I observed Moriarty's impassive eyes blink. 'We know all that. The question I was about to put to the Professor is, why?'

Moriarty returned him an uncomprehending stare.

'*Why*, Professor? Why do you do it? Why devote the resources of one of the world's most remarkable brains to manipulating an organization of criminals to no apparent purpose. What – and I ask purely from curiosity, not in any attempt to entrap you – what causes a man of good birth and excellent education, endowed by Nature with a phenomenal mathematical faculty, who, at the age of twenty-one wrote a treatise upon the Binomial Theorem which had a European vogue...'

'*Has*,' corrected Moriarty, in a leaden tone which carried neither triumph nor pride.

'... whose study, *The Dynamics of an Asteroid*, I have heard it said, ascends to the most rarefied heights of pure mathematics. What, I ask in all sincerity, is your purpose, your motive in life?'

I found myself holding my breath, awaiting eagerly the answer to this audacious question which perhaps none but my brother, with his omnipotent standing, would have asked; but no response came. Moriarty's deeply hooded eyes may well have been shut, for all I could see. Only his great head moved, to and fro.

Mycroft did not let up. 'I know as much as anyone in this world about you, Professor Moriarty; more even than my brother, for all his special interest in you. Like him, I know you to be a man of ascetic habits, not subject to the weaknesses and vices which are common in at least some degree to most men. You have immense wealth, spread among perhaps twenty banks, the bulk of them outside England, yet you continue to coach dullards for army commissions for an income which I have ascertained amounts to only some seven hundred pounds a year. Where is it all leading?'

The silence in that gloomy, panelled room was as dense as the shadows around us. There was not movement enough to cause even the candles' yellow spears to waver.

At long last, Moriarty's eyelids twitched and raised enough to disclose the eyes beneath them. They seemed to have retreated even more deeply into those twin caverns under the massive overhang of brow, and I thought I had never seen so melancholy a look on human features.

His lips scarcely moved as he murmured his reply: 'Where everything leads to, of course. For the worst and best of us, it all comes to the same.'

Rarefied Heights

No CLOCK ticked its solemn strokes in the Committee Room, and the street sounds did not penetrate to where Mycroft and I sat opposite one another at the table, still and unspeaking, as we watched the ceaseless movements of that bowed, skull-like dome.

At long last the hooded eyebrows twitched and lifted, uncovering that penetrating gaze which, by the head's motion, was swung to and fro from one to the other of us.

'My so-called academic colleagues resented me,' he said, in a voice so low that I had to check myself from leaning forward to attune to it. I did not wish to miss a word, yet feared, by so little as an eye's flicker, to interrupt, and perhaps terminate, a statement which all my senses told me was to be one which he had never made in his life before – had not even, perhaps, allowed his conscious mind to acknowledge.

He had paused, and when he spoke again it was to repeat himself, with an emphasis born out of a bitterness which was clearly heartfelt.

' "Resented"? "Hated" would be a better term for their contempt for one who was so obviously head and shoulders above them in intellect; who had achieved and published results which they could not have hoped to rival in a hundred lifetimes. It is something they are incapable of admiring, and can never forgive. Had I joined in their cliques and coteries, it would have been different. In that way, they are able to make themselves aware of everything one is doing. Should one strike out upon some original line of research, they ascertain all they can of one's results and publish them hastily under their own names. The conclusions are not complete, of course, but so nearly so that when one does complete them, those parasites can assert that the entire groundwork had been done by them, that they had been on the very brink of publishing, even, and accuse one of stealing the results which they themselves had already filched from under one's very nose.

'At first, I imagine, they merely scoffed at me. Their animosity was vain irritation that I, a youth of not yet one-and-twenty at the time, could have the presumption to keep my work apart from them, my elders and "betters", instead of fawning to them for condescension and advice. They became positively indignant when I refused the information. I was given to understand, in the form of hints, that my place at the university was in some jeopardy.

'I took no heed, and carried on in my own way. Then I discovered the extent that note was being taken of what books and papers I had been withdrawing from the library, and of those less easily obtainable ones for which I had had to request the Librarian to send away. It was a useful lesson in life, in more ways than one. It showed me to what lengths men of high reputation and supposedly impeccable character will go – and it also taught me the value of keeping one's tracks covered.'

I fancied I caught the tiniest spark of amusement in his eyes as they chanced to meet mine at the one extreme of their repetitious arc. If so, it was for the merest instance, and there was no lessening of the bitterness as he went on.

'But my game was already up, to some extent. They must have learned that it was the binomial theorem which was preoccupying me, for among the books obtained for me was the first volume of *Crelle's Journal* of 1826, whose chief entry is the Norwegian, Abel's, immensely long and most thorough proof of the theorem, as adduced in elementary form in Bernoulli's *Ars conjectandi*, published posthumously in 1713, and more generally by Euler.

'Thus far they had been able to trace my footsteps, and I could imagine their smug satisfaction that there could be no further forward for me to go on my solitary exploration. I foresaw myself, with one mighty bound, soaring high above the heads of those ineffectual dons whom I knew had nothing to teach me and were my superiors only by virtue of their position in the university.

'I proceeded to outwit them. While laying a smokescreen, as it were, by re-ordering those eighteenth-century works of which I have spoken, I sought to give the impression that I had run up against obstacles which had driven me back to retrace

SHERLOCK HOLMES: MY LIFE AND CRIMES

ground already covered, and to puzzle anew to find a way beyond the limits of those early studies. However, I equipped myself with credentials which persuaded the trustees of the British Museum that, although under age, I was a fit person to use the Reading Room. I immured myself there, and went back to Pascal's treatise of 1665, and beyond that to a Chinese tract by Chu Shih-Chieh, dating as early as 1303.

'To cut the story short, with the complete historical progression of study into the search for a theorem for the raising of a binomial at my fingertips, I found it easy to trace the way to Sir Isaac Newton's result of 1676, prove it to my own satisfaction, and demonstrate to what extent later proofs are valid.'

'Remarkable, Professor! You agree, Sherlock, I am sure.'

'Absolutely!' I seconded him, and even got a pale shade of a nod of appreciation from the glistening dome wherein such undoubted brain-power reposed.

'You published your results, and confounded your dons, I take it?'

The cold eyes glistened with re-lived triumph.

'I did. What is more, as a precaution against tampering with my manuscript, or worse, I arranged publication not through my own university's press, but through that of the smaller establishment which, as doubtless you know, awarded me its chair of mathematics on the strength of it. It was a sort of *quid pro quo*. The treatise appeared after I had joined that second university, so that, in the eyes of all Europe, it was seen to be the patron of my work, and took the prestige. There was some faint protest from the other place, but it was ignored. And that was sweet – sweet!'

He was not going to find life so sweet that coming Monday, I mused. The breaking of his organization, towards which I had worked patiently and diligently for years, was going to leave him with a very sour taste indeed.

Or so I thought, as we three sat there in that long, dark, candle-flickering room, with a fresh charge of that silken brandy before each of us, and Mycroft casually picking the band off a cigar, letting the pause in our conversation hang suspended to allow us to digest the course just finished, before proceeding to the next.

'You had won your academic battle, Professor Moriarty,' Mycroft continued at last. 'Was that not enough?'

68

Moriarty was silent for some moments before answering.

'For me, perhaps it would have been – should have been. It was they who would not give over. As you are aware, the groves of academe are thronged with bitter, frustrated non-entities who begrudge anyone the success which has gained him notice such as has never come their way. They exercise their spite individually and *en masse*. In my case it went true to pattern: they closed ranks against me.'

'In what ways?'

'Oh, difficulties arising wherever difficulty could arise; obstructions; whispers that the inspiration behind my paper had not been mine at all, but that of a fellow worker outside the university, over whom I had influence enough to keep his name suppressed. I was a bachelor who took no part in sporting or social activities – who had, to put it baldly, no association with the female sex and an alleged disinclination towards any. You can imagine the vile sort of rumours which began to be spread about the form of my influence over this purported colleague of mine.'

The Reading Room of the British Museum, opened in 1857. Under its mighty dome I gained much of the knowledge required for my profession and to enable me to write my monographs. Professor Moriarty had also been an avid user of this library of a million volumes.

'Which, of course, you could not take steps to refute without running the risk of drawing further attention to them, and making it seem that where smoke was, there might be fire?'

'Precisely. In all likelihood, there was no conspiracy, as such. It was simply a classic case of the assassination of character being conducted by common assent and motives.'

'Were you not able to recognize it as such, and discount it?'

'I had been brought up to believe that to move in academic circles was a privilege any man might treasure, and that to make your mark in them was to qualify for respect and esteem. Besides, while the whispers against me were mounting towards that point where they would become positively dangerous my mind was concentrated on other things. I was deeply engaged in my studies into the asteroid. Nothing so ambitious had ever been undertaken before. When you consider the honours, the rewards, the popular acclamation which are regularly heaped upon men whose attainments are trivial and ephemeral, compared with mine. . .!'

His voice had risen during this last sentence, which broke off on a high-pitched, indignant note, quite different from his customary low and oily tone. He put up the closed fingers of one long, white hand to his brow, as if in an effort to check the oscillations from becoming more violent.

My brother, who had been careful to give all his attention to him, took the opportunity to flick a brief glance towards me. I read caution in it. He was warning me – unnecessarily, as it happened – that this singular interview was nearing some point of crisis, which one interruption out of place could spoil. What his greater game was, of course, I still did not know. How he had got Moriarty to come here, into what might have proved a trap, and tolerate the company of myself, the man whom he counted his arch enemy, as I so counted him, it was beyond me to comprehend. Mycroft's ways were ever mysterious, though, and his sources of information perhaps greater than those of anyone in the kingdom, the Prime Minister not excepted.

It was my task to do nothing, save sit absolutely still and quiet, unnoticed as near as possible to the point of invisibility, while Mycroft played his game to its end.

With a suddenness which almost made me jump, Moriarty withdrew his hand from his brow, jerked up his head, and snapped at Mycroft. 'The rest must be obvious. You must draw from it your own conclusions, however. I admit nothing.'

His defiant glare included me this time, seeming to be tempting some challenge which he would loftily refuse. Mycroft claimed his attention again, though.

'Professor Moriarty, you have been good enough so far to tell a story which I find wholly credible and sincere. You are a man of excellent background and education, possessed of phenomenal – I would go so far as to hazard unique – mental powers. You first demonstrated those powers to the world at large with your *Treatise on the Binomial Theorem*, which brought down on you the jealousy and odium of colleagues to whom you had looked for acclaim. That bitter disappointment had been compensated for to some extent by your winning an appointment to a chair of mathematics at a relatively early age, and by the satisfaction of having "cocked your snook" over those who had tried to stand in your way.

'You brushed off the bitterness so far as you were able, in order to concentrate all your faculties upon this further study which could bring you world renown. Your opponents redoubled their efforts against you, however, and, through

A ceremonial procession of Oxford University dons. This outward show of academic fellowship conceals a seething tumult of rivalries, jealousies, conspiracies and malicious resentments, as Moriarty found in university circles. Such influences were too intense for his innate paranoia, driving him to crime.

The Thames and Victoria Embankment with New Scotland Yard on the right and Big Ben and the Houses of Parliament beyond. My inexcusable blunder led to young John Openshaw being decoyed to a spot near here and drowned in the case of THE FIVE ORANGE PIPS *in 1887.*

innuendo which would have been found to be slanderous, had you taken steps to prove it, provoked the university authorities to deprive you of your chair.'

'There *were* no steps that I could take!' Moriarty almost shouted, so that the lofty spaces of the room rang. 'No proof that would satisfy the law, and what other remedy does a victim have? If he takes the law into his own hands he is . . .' He broke off sharply. I had no doubt in that moment that when the full extent of the Moriarty gang's record was gradually uncovered a number of outstanding mysteries concerning men in academic circles who had met with ruin and worse would be solved. In some way, they would prove to be men whose careers had points of coincidence with Moriarty's own, though all the odds were that nothing would be found to link his name with the causes of their subsequent misfortunes.

'We will say no more of that, Professor,' Mycroft was replying. 'Suffice it that you lost your chair, and your occupation, and were compelled to come to London, and seek your living as an army coach.'

'That is my profession,' Moriarty answered carefully. 'Let him who suggests otherwise watch his step.'

'Quite, quite,' said Mycroft hastily. 'But *The Dynamics of an Asteroid* – that was published after your final departure from university life, I understand?'

'Published, and ignored.'

'Ignored? Come, come, Professor – as I understand it, it has not been so much ignored, as that there exists no one capable of comprehending it sufficiently to review it or comment on it.'

'They understand neither the connection between the dynamics of asteroids and the dynamics of atoms, nor the link which I demonstrated between classical dynamics and electro-dynamics. So they pretend that the whole work is incomprehensible. By doing that, they hope it will remain overlooked until some other isolated genius, who happens to be more congenial to them, comes along and *is* able to convince them that $E = mc^2$. Then they will happily acclaim his as the finest brain in the world.

'But the hour is getting very late indeed, Mr Mycroft Holmes. Thanks to your brother here. I have a busy weekend before me, preparing to defend myself against the worst he can do me. I will bid you good night – or rather, by now, good morning.'

I had begun instinctively to rise, as he did, but Mycroft's great bulk remained unmoving in his chair. He waved a podgy hand, between whose first two fingers his thick cigar had half burned away.

'Please sit down, Professor. You are under no restraint, I hasten to assure you; but the business on which I invited you to come here has scarcely begun.'

ESCAPE TO THE CONTINENT

'...It would be a great pleasure to me, therefore, if you could come on to the Continent with me.'

'The practice is quiet, and I have an accommodating neighbour. I should be glad to come.'

Dear old Watson and his accommodating neighbour! I almost fancy he had more of them than he had patients, for he always proved able to join me, whether it was on a journey or in answer to a summons to meet me at once at Goldini's Restaurant, Gloucester Road, and fetch with him 'a jemmy, a dark lantern, a chisel and a revolver'. He was similarly fortunate in his successive wives – or, in a sense, I was. I was never denied his company in an adventure; though, to do myself justice, I believe I never sought it unreasonably.

So now, here he was again, with his doggy eyes lighting up at the prospect of an outing, though showing also his concern for my safety. I had told him how the Moriarty gang were trying to close in on me to forestall the vital evidence I had in readiness to give against them. As I had pointed out to Mycroft last evening, when he gave me my instructions to leave the country forthwith, Watson might think it uncharacteristic of me to run from danger, but Mycroft had insisted.

'Spare no pains to make him see the urgency of it. Put on that pale, thin look of yours when you call on him, and contrive to tremble a little. Beg him to draw his shutters against any possible observer outside, and puff a nervous cigarette. Oh, and it would be a nice touch to give that damaged fist of yours a good rasp against a rough wall beforehand. Show him the blood, and tell him how you just shook off "four rogues in buckram".'

I laughed at that, but Mycroft shook his head seriously.

'I am not being flippant, Sherlock. Ironically, in this instance, your greatest friend poses the chief risk to our enterprise.

Of all persons on earth (I except myself, as a special case) he is the one who can be counted upon to be so shocked and stricken by your demise as to insist on its investigation to the full. There are those who are aware of that, and will watch him closely, anxious to share in any discoveries he might make. He must be seen to give up his inquiries as hopeless, genuinely convinced that there is nowhere further for them to lead. The sorrowing account which he will undoubtedly publish to the world will carry more conviction and finality than any *Times* obituary.'

'Poor Watson. It's going to be hardest on him.'

'You rib him often enough, and play your little tricks at his expense, but you know his true worth. He is too honest to lie convincingly, and, I'm sure you will agree, too naive to keep a secret, should any suspicious party determine to wheedle it out of him.'

'Well, I suppose it must be so. It will be hard enough for me to dissemble to him. At any rate, it will give his wife her chance to show whatever it is wives are supposed to be capable of at such times.'

Such were the circumstances leading to the dramatic events which, in Watson's chronicle, shook the world. His published account represents what he believed to be the unvarnished truth, and I hereby testify that not a word of what he wrote was other than what happened – *in so far as he was allowed to perceive it.*

I presented myself abruptly at his consulting-room late on that following evening of Friday, 24 April, and startled him by edging my way round his walls, to close the window shutters without asking his by-your-leave. I explained that I was afraid for my life, showing him burst and bleeding knuckles in testimony to having just beaten off one attempt.

Puffing gratefully at a cigarette, I embarked upon the farrago of deception, telling him that I had been visited at Baker Street that morning by the 'Napoleon of Crime' in person, to warn me of the consequences of the trouble I was causing him.

' "It has been a duel between you and me, Mr Holmes," ' went my report. ' "You hope to place me in the dock. I tell you that I will never stand in the dock. You hope to beat me. If you are clever enough to bring destruction upon me, rest assured that I shall do as much to you." '

'"You have paid me several compliments, Mr Moriarty. Let me pay you one in return when I say that if I were assured of the former eventuality, I would, in the interests of the public, cheerfully accept the latter."

'"I can promise you the one but not the other," ' he snarled, and so turned his rounded back upon me and went peering and blinking out of the room.'

I went on to tell Watson of the several attempts on my life, and asked him to come away with me until after the completion of the police round-up, which could not take place before Monday. Naturally, he agreed without hesitation, at which I proceeded to instruct him precisely what to do, in accordance with what Mycroft, in previous turn, had instructed me. Then I took an exaggeratedly cautious leave by scrambling over his back garden wall.

Next day's charade worked perfectly. Watson had sent his luggage ahead of him to Victoria Station. He himself was to take a hansom to the Strand entrance of the Lowther Arcade, through which he must dash on foot to the far end, where he would find waiting a small brougham, driven by a fellow with a heavy black cloak, tipped at the collar with red. (In fact, he was a well-muffled Mycroft, who was anxious to ensure that

Victoria Station in London, from where Watson and I began our journey to Switzerland in 1891. The rival London Chatham & Dover and South Eastern railways operated between them a complex network in Southern England, and our circuitous journey to escape Moriarty's pursuit involved using both.

all went well.) It would take Watson to Victoria, in time for the Continental express. His luggage would be aboard, and he would find a reserved first-class compartment, the second from the front of the train, which would be our rendezvous.

I watched him approaching along the platform with his porter, glancing about for sight of me. Not seeing me, he allowed the porter to usher him into the carriage, where I promptly joined him. The chagrin and dismay which he displayed at this was explicable from my disguise as a venerable Italian priest, in shovel hat and soutane. Watson's and the porter's protests were wasted on my uncomprehending ears, as I fussed about my own luggage and settled myself determinedly in a seat. Whistles were blowing, doors slamming shut, including ours, and I heard Watson's groan as the train jerked into motion, with no sign of his intended companion.

'My dear Watson,' I said, 'You have not even condescended to say good morning.'

My reward, as always when I perpetrated such little tricks on him, was the comical open mouth of astonishment, followed by the suspicious peer of disbelief, and finally the slapped thigh and outburst of relieved and admiring laughter. But I beckoned him urgently to the window, for there was something I required him to see. It was a tall man, pushing his way through the crowd, waving his hand as if expecting the train to stop for him. It only gathered speed, leaving him standing.

Watson looked at me inquiringly.

'Moriarty himself,' I said grimly. 'You see how, for all our precautions, he is hot on our trail. Confound it, after I had taken such pains to disappear until it is all over.'

'But we've shaken him off. This express connects directly with the Dover boat.'

'My dear Watson,' I said, ridding myself of my disguise, 'do you think that if I were the pursuer, and Moriarty my pursued, I should let a little difficulty like that get in my way? I should be at this moment in the station-master's office, engaging a special train to follow us.'

'A special! But . . . think of the organization! A locomotive and carriage to get ready. Arrangements to be made all along the line to let it through. We shall be at Dover in two hours . . .'

'With at least a fifteen minutes' wait for the boat to leave,' I reminded him, 'not to mention stops at Herne Hill, Chatham and Canterbury, each with its risk of unanticipated delays. No, it is too risky. 'We must sacrifice our baggage by letting it go on to Paris, while we ourselves alight at Canterbury and make our way to Newhaven. It will mean a weary and circuitous journey, but unless I am mistaken there is a night boat from there to Dieppe. We can get a train from there to Brussels.'

I saw Watson's jaw sink lower at all this, and guessed why: he had foreseen our journey in terms of a series of successively improving meals to be leisurely enjoyed, at well regulated intervals. A whole day's detour around southeastern England, culminating at Newhaven, must have been a distinctly less alluring prospect.

It was no pleasure to me to torment my trusty companion, in whose company I had so little time left to spend; but Mycroft had insisted that the more pains I appeared to be at to evade Moriarty's pursuit, the more thoroughly convinced Watson would be that every detail of the worst excursion of his lifetime had occurred genuinely. It was vital that he should.

So we got down at Canterbury, where we found a stopping connection to Ashford, which would connect with another slow service to Hastings, thence by another to Lewes, and yet one more to Newhaven, a weary progress totalling nearly six hours, as against our originally anticipated two. Watson sustained himself unhappily with cups of railway tea and such broken victuals as he could find on station counters, wherever there was time.

Our only moment of drama was during our first and longest wait, at Canterbury. Our own train had barely vanished from sight before a distantly approaching rumble caught my ear and I looked up the line to see a curl of smoke. I pulled Watson back behind a pile of luggage on the platform, from where we saw the pursuing special fly through, whistle shrieking.

'There he goes,' I remarked. 'Hot-foot for Paris.'

'I could envy him,' Watson said ruefully.

The time wanted some twenty minutes till noon. I glanced up at the enamelled BUFFET sign. 'We have a good half-hour to wait. The question is whether we should take a premature lunch here, or run our risk of starving before we reach the buffet at Newhaven.'

'That is one risk I prefer not to run, Holmes,' he replied, and resolutely led the way in.

DINNER AT THE ENGLISCHER HOF

WATSON'S DECISION had been shrewd, for it was to prove many more hours before the solace of a fully set table, an ample menu, and a beaming head waiter were to be his. That was in Brussels, on Sunday evening, having left London at breakfast time on Saturday. I began to wonder if Mycroft's strategy had not be a trifle over-elaborate.

We lingered briefly in the Belgian capital, then moved on to Strasbourg. There I found a telegram awaiting me. It was from Scotland Yard, reporting the complete success of the operation against Moriarty's organization, though regretting that the spider himself had apparently abandoned his web in good time, leaving no trace of his whereabouts. This was indeed 'regretable', and the implications clear.

It was my cue to address my companion seriously.

'I think you had better return to England, Watson.'

'Alone? Why?'

'Because you will find me a dangerous companion now. This man's occupation is gone. He is lost if he returns to London. He threatened to devote his energies to revenging himself on me, and I have no doubt that he meant it. I should certainly recommend you to return to your practice and your wife.'

Of course, he refused.

'I shall go when you go, Holmes. As to this Moriarty, who is probably scouring Paris for you still, from what you say he will scarcely dare show his face in London again. My suggestion is that we make the most of a few days of Swiss air and food – which, speaking as a doctor, I strongly advocate for your run-down condition – and then make our way homeward through Holland and Harwich. For my money, you've seen the last of that gentleman.'

Following a brief show of argument, I acquiesced, and that same night we were well on our way to Geneva.

We spent a week wandering the Valley of the Rhône. It was Watson who broke the idea of branching off at Leuk and crossing the snow-deep Gemmi Pass, though it clearly did not register with him that it was a hint of mine which had put it into his mind. As he recorded later, with heavy-hearted recollection, it was a lovely trip, 'the dainty green of the spring below, the virgin white of the winter above'. But it was my heart which weighed leaden then, at the thought of how soon this best of friends who strode beside me, making light of such discomfort as his old wound must have been causing him, was destined to be plunged into grief and desolation.

Although the Englischer Hof hotel at Meiringen, where Watson and I stayed in 1891, escaped the fire which destroyed much of the village later that year, it was burned down not long after my later residence there with 'Etherage' in 1894 and I have no photographs of it. It quite closely resembled this other typically Swiss country hotel.

At Interlaken, I suggested we make for Meiringen, which our guide book recommended as a quaint old-world gem of traditional cottages nestling about a fine little church of the pre-Reformation period. A hotel named the Englischer Hof sounded comfortingly inviting. It proved even more so to Watson when we were greeted on its porch by an avuncular-mannered old landlord, who told us in excellent English that he had served three years at the Grosvenor Hotel in the Buckingham Palace Road. He introduced himself as Peter Steiler, the elder.

'I took the earliest opportunity to talk to him alone, while Watson was upstairs unpacking in his room.

'He passed through two days ago,' he told me without needing to be asked. 'He is at Rosenlaui. While the weather remains so good, I suggest you do not delay.'

'When do you propose, then?'

'Tomorrow afternoon. If you agree, I will send him word immediately.'

'Agreed. Steiler...'

'Herr Holmes?'

'Dr Watson... He has been my closest friend.'

The old eyes softened.

'I understand. I will do all I can for him.'

'Including the best dinner this evening of which your chef is capable – since it's to be our last together.'

Steiler's chef, who happened to be his wife, rose magnificently to the occasion with a succession of regional dishes, each with its appropriate wine. At one point I almost had cause to regret my injunction to our host.

'My word!' Watson exclaimed, dabbing heavily at his lips with the huge napkin, which the ever-watchful waiter rushed forward to replace with a fresh one. 'I don't know when I ate like this. I vote we make a few days of it here.'

I thought swiftly.

'I was having a chat with old Steiler. He tells me we must on no account leave this part without going up to view the Falls of Reichenbach. They're at their most spectacular just now, with the melting snow, and with the weather so unpredictable in the mountains we should lose no time going there.'

Watson pulled a face. 'Can't we nip up in the morning, and be back here again for dinner?'

'If we carry on upward, the track takes us over to Rosenlaui, our next stage. Steiler sends all his travellers on to the inn there. There's a friendly rivalry between his wife and the good lady at Rosenlaui as to who collects the most compliments for her table.'

'Oho! In that case . . .'

The fateful day, 4 May, dawned fine and clear, all silver and white, with merest trails of gossamer cloud hanging motionless about the peaks. I saw the dawn, having abandoned fruitless attempts to sleep after the early hours. I stood long at my window, puffing my pipe while Nature displayed her wondrous transformation scene for my benefit.

Watson's contented snores droned steadily in the adjoining room. For years I had worked to proof my heart against emotion of any kind. It was, in a slight sense, comforting to find that I had not succeeded so thoroughly as to have become wholly incapable of feeling. I believe it was distaste that was uppermost in me just then; that self-contempt which any man with the least spark of decency in him must feel when he has determined, for whatever reason, to cut himself off from his parents, leave his wife, or abandon his dog by some roadside, telling it to sit obediently and wait for his return, which he has made up his mind shall not take place.

There was good reason to harbour emotions on my own behalf of a very different sort. If things were to go awry, Watson's forthcoming grief could be all too justified. More than once I picked up my small revolver and weighed it in my palm, reassuring myself of its balance. I spun the chamber, as I had done a dozen times, watching for that hesitation which would indicate the speck of dirt which could prove disastrous when it came to snapping off a desperate second shot. It spun easily every time.

It came as a relief at last to hear the bustling sounds of the Steilers and their servants preparing for the day. We had arranged to set off after luncheon, implying a long drag of a morning, terminated by an early meal, to permit us a short rest before setting off up the steep track leading to Rosenlaui, from which a brief detour would take us to view the waterfall.

'Goodbye, Steiler,' I said to him aside, as I shook his hand.

'Good luck, Herr Holmes.' His eyes searched mine; but mine had nothing to tell him in return.

I let Watson lead the way, to make the pace with his gammy leg. We climbed steadily, only speaking whenever we paused to turn and survey the view. There was no snow at this level, merely rock and thin earth beneath our feet. After a little over half an hour a distant rumbling reached our ears simultaneously.

'The Falls?' Watson asked.

'I fancy so. Steiler said there is a distinct branch off the path.'

We soon came to it. Now the tumbling of the cascade had mounted to a boom, and all at once to a roar, as we rounded a bend of the new track and found ourselves confronted by a great downward rush of green water, projected over a jagged lip of black rock. As we edged closer, a curtain of spray veered towards us, wetting our faces and clothes.

We went as near the edge as we dared venture, craning our necks to look down into the boiling chasm far below. It was a terrible place indeed, and I was not sorry to see that the track, which had been deliberately cut to afford a viewpoint, ended abruptly with a rock face, preventing further progress.

The noise was too great for conversation; indeed, what could there have been to remark that was not fatuously obvious? We exchanged a nod, and turned back towards the main pathway. We were equally startled, therefore, to hear what was undoubtedly a human cry. We halted as one and saw a stumbling form, in Swiss mountain clothing, making as much haste as possible, with the aid of an alpenstock. He was calling, 'Herr Doktor! Herr Doktor!'

He was a young lad, whom we did not recognize. He reached us, panting heavily, and drew from his pocket a crumpled sheet of notepaper, which I noticed bore the emblem of the Englischer Hof. Watson seized it, and read aloud:

Herr Doktor

   Half an hour after you left, an English lady arrived at the hotel from Davos Platz on her way to friends at Lucerne. She has consumption and has collapsed in my hotel. She begs for an English doctor, but there is not one in Meiringen. She fears she might die. I beg you, please come to her as a favour to

   Yours truly
   P. Steiler (Landlord)

'You speak English?' Watson addressed the youth loudly.

'Ja, ja, I speak. Herr Steiler is mein Onkel. Long time in London.'

'Why did he not summon a Swiss doctor?'

'Ja, ja, he has! Aber, the lady is crying, und saying she will some other English see before she die.'

'Sounds serious, Holmes.'

'You must go, Watson, that is plain.'

'Well, it's unthinkable to refuse such a request. But you'll come down with me?'

'If you won't mind, I think I'd prefer to stay here and ponder this magnificent sight a while. There is nothing I can do to help. I will give you an hour or so, and then stroll slowly on towards Rosenlaui, and expect to see you on the way or when you can get there. At the worst, you'll be able to stay for another of Frau Steiler's dinners after all.'

He grinned. 'No, no. I'll join up with you. Calm this lady down, and persuade her she'll be just as well cared for in Swiss hands.'

'Please . . . ?' urged the anxious lad.

'All right,' said Watson. 'I'm coming. Adieu for the moment, Holmes.'

'Adieu . . . my dear Watson.'

He was already stumbling down the path after the fleeter-footed boy, too concerned about watching his step to turn round and wave.

I waved, nevertheless, and stood and watched him out of sight, before turning and, with my back against the sheer cliff face and my arms folded, resuming my scrutiny of that relentless torrent, hurling itself far beneath me.

For perhaps fifteen minutes I stood, half-mesmerized by the movement of the water, the tricks of light against the misty spray, and the relentless noise. Then instinct made me turn sharply – and not a yard away a tall, gaunt figure stood, long arms hanging free at its sides, skull-like head bare, and deep, baleful eyes regarding me with a gaze which never wavered, although the head oscillated ceaselessly from side to side.

THE MEETING AT THE
REICHENBACH FALLS

He ADVANCED very slowly, just the three or so paces needed to bring him within arm's reach of me. My grip on my alpenstock tightened, and it took the strength of my arm, as well as my nerve, to keep it forced down by my side. His cold eyes were on mine, their pupils moving slightly to compensate for the oscillation of his head.

He had one hand in the pocket of his black English overcoat, with fur collar. I could not judge whether it gripped a revolver, but expected as much.

'Well, Mr Holmes,' was all his greeting.

'Professor Moriarty,' I acknowledged simply.

'I see that you have been as good – or should I say as bad? – as your word,' he went on. 'The newspapers report a spate of arrests in London.'

'All of men to whom the name Professor Moriarty is quite unknown, I expect.'

He regarded me unblinkingly. 'Why should it be known? What had any of them to do with me, or I with them?'

'For all that the police and the courts will find out – nothing. Your methods run ahead of that sort of thing, Professor.'

He gave me a chilly smile, as if to say he had nothing to add, and the subject was closed. He gazed about.

'So, we pitch our ring here?'

I had examined the ground while I waited. A few paces from where we stood a vein of black soil emerged from the rock and spread out across it, kept perpetually muddy by the spray from the torrent. Watson's and my footprints were clearly imprinted in it. I motioned towards it with the alpenstock. Moriarty's arm twitched instinctively at my move, confirming

my suspicion that he held a revolver ready for instant use; but he took in my meaning, and pointedly withdrew the hand from his pocket empty.

'Both of us must enter that mud patch and register our prints,' I told him. 'Neither must appear to return.'

'It will be a temptation to one of us, if not both,' he answered, almost skittishly.

'We must make only two or three clear steps each,' I instructed. 'It will be possible to walk backwards again in exact register with them, taking the greatest care. Too many prints would increase the margin of error.'

'By the time a police expert is brought here it will have been trampled into a morass,' he snorted.

I shook my head. 'My friend Watson will perhaps be first on the scene, and he knows my methods. It is imperative that he should notice the different sets of footprints – his and mine entering the mud patch, over which we walked in order to look down into the Fall, and returning again, but yours and mine entering only.'

'You seem to hold his intelligence in high regard.'

'Watson is no fool, let me assure you. It is largely because of it that this charade is necessary. If there is one man in the world who is going to rack his brains over what has happened, he is that one.'

'Well, then, what else must there be for this paragon to discover?'

'The marks of our struggle. The mud must be churned to the very edge of the abyss . . .'

'Allow me to invite you to enjoy that privilege,' Moriarty smiled unpleasantly. 'Your foot might slip, and my conscience would be quite clear.'

I gave him a hard stare.

'Professor, if you will be good enough to take three paces on to the mud patch, then stand still, I will guide you precisely back. Then I will follow your example, and do what else is necessary before returning.'

The Reichenbach Falls near Meiringen where Moriarty and I met for our 'struggle to the death' on May 4, 1891. As my pages will reveal, the circumstances and aftermath were vastly different from those chronicled by poor Watson in his narrative THE FINAL PROBLEM.

It was his turn to contemplate me. It was not difficult to read his thoughts: one hard thrust from my alpenstock into his back as he stepped towards the abyss, and the Napoleon of Crime would be no more. No one would know that he had even been with me there: even Mycroft would have to believe whatever version I chose to give him of what had happened. I might consider my mission of so many years complete at last.

I turned and flung the alpenstock some yards behind me along the ledge, and spread my empty hands towards him, hesitating there. With a grunt of acceptance, he turned his back on me and proceeded to take three careful paces with each foot to within a matter of eighteen inches from a plunge to oblivion. . . .

I guided him backwards, ensuring that the soles of his boots fitted precisely the prints he had registered. If he still mistrusted me, he did not show it. While carrying out the task he had not glanced round once, nor cocked his ear to catch warning of any movement by me. I kept quite still, to reassure him, and directed him back towards me by my voice alone.

Now it was my turn. As I steadied myself to take the first careful step forward, I was conscious of him just behind me. Great though my temptation had been to push him over the edge, his must have been immeasurably more so. If he were to dispatch me, he could afford to let his old organization go hang – as some of its members undoubtedly would, after Monday's police coup. He could melt away into Europe or elsewhere, recruiting a new gang, and resume his evil career.

Three factors emboldened me to take that step towards the precipice knowing that I was safe from him. One was that remarkable narrative which I had listened to in London, followed later by some further conversation between my brother and myself after Moriarty had left us.

My second assurance of security was the arrangement which brought us to this precise part of a mountain ledge where, it was soon to be supposed, we had fought one another to the death. Moriarty had made his bargain with Mycroft, and we were both of us convinced that he meant to keep it – although far from sure what we might expect him to do afterwards.

Finally, there was the knowledge, which Moriarty and I shared, that should he attempt to leave that mountain pass alone, by either end (there was no intermediate way out of it) he would never succeed. Both the Englischer Hof in Meiringen, and its equivalent establishment up at Rosenlaui, had a guest staying at present whose most important item of baggage was a locked case containing, in separate components, a high-powered rifle. Neither of these marksmen knew the identity of his prospective quarry, only his description. They were under Mycroft's personal orders to be in position this after-noon. If either should see that unmistakable figure attempting to leave the mountain alone, he must shoot him dead.

When Mycroft had told Moriarty this contingency plan, in my hearing, the response had been a cold smile, and the wry inquiry whether the same arrangement stood in my own case; but the point had been taken.

Only Watson – the loyal, goodhearted Watson, the one to whom it was rightly owed to be trusted to play some part in all this – was to be kept totally in the dark. His role was that of dupe, and his reward for playing it was to be left to grieve, so that he would convey that grief convincingly to the world.

Having registered my footprints in the spongy black soil I did not at once retreat. I stepped even further towards the lip of the abyss, to screw my boot soles into the furthermost part of the surface, giving the appearance of a struggle having taken place there. I beat down the sparse brambles and fern which grew in the rock face, to look as though a man's body had been forced against them in the course of that struggle. I ventured to the very edge of the drop and gingerly, with one foot, broke away a portion of the overhang, which went tumbling into the torrent in a manner which was enough to make me shudder.

I was glad to complete my task, watched all the time by Moriarty, his hands deep in his coat pockets against the cold, only his head moving. Then I made my careful retreat, needing no guidance from him where to set my feet exactly to match my existing prints. It was an old trick which I had used in the past, far more efficient than reversing the boots by strapping them beneath another pair. The mark of the strap itself was all too likely to show itself in the surface, besides which any ex-pert observer could gauge from the complete imprint that it had been made by an abnormal distribution of the weight upon the feet.

'Well done, Mr Holmes, well done!' Moriarty congratulated me in a mocking tone, when I stood beside him again, surveying my work. 'If I may say so, the criminal profession has lost a master practitioner in you.'

'In order to guard against being deceived, it is necessary to be *au fait* with all methods of committing deceit, Professor.'

'It is strange, is it not, that an identical set of accomplishments should be capable of being used for precisely the opposite purpose? Do you suppose that we, as individuals, have the free choice of which use we shall put them to – or does predestiny come into it?'

'I believe we are the subjects of our circumstances. Some of us become their victims; others master them. As to whether that surrender or mastery is due to our natures, or is forced on us by some power greater than ourselves, or whether the choice is ours to make from our free will, I am afraid I am unable to answer. The only certainty I have to offer at this moment is that it is time we were getting away from here before Watson comes back, or someone else sees us.'

I walked to where my fallen alpenstock lay and retrieved it. I propped the stick against the rock wall and left it there.

'Permit me to go first, Professor,' I suggested. 'I fancy my methods of working have accustomed my senses to be keener than yours. If anyone else chances to be upon this path, and I give the word, get at once into whatever cover you can and stay completely still until they are out of sight again. It is imperative that we are not seen together.'

He nodded, and we set off at a brisk pace on the upward slope of the track. No one was in sight, and we had not far to go before the path began to broaden and become less steep, leaving the mountain edge to wind along the foot of a steep-sided valley, with abundant growth all about. From the heart of London, Mycroft had planned the whole thing immaculately. I knew that somewhere in that bracken his sharpshooter lay, watching us go by, his mission accomplished without needing to pull his trigger.

Before long we crested a rise and saw the village of Rosenlaui below us. As I had been instructed, a fork in the track soon appeared. We took that arm of it which branched away from the village, and quickened our step on the downward incline, intent on putting as many miles as possible between us and the

Falls of Reichenbach before Watson's discovery should become news.

Much of our trek was through the long dusk, and then in darkness. Our path was little frequented, with no tourists about and the country folk presumably indoors for the night. Only once did we have to conceal ourselves. We did a good ten miles, by my reckoning, before I called a halt.

Moriarty, who had kept up well for a man some eight years my senior and of misleadingly frail physique, grumbled a little at the notion of having to spend the night under the stars; but he knew the arrangement, and had to accept it, making himself as comfortable as he could by enveloping himself in the army blanket which he had brought in the small valise which was all the luggage he had with him. I had my rucksack, having had to leave the rest of my baggage at the Englischer Hof, to be forwarded with Watson's to our next planned destination, Lucerne. I had brought with me only essentials for that night – a blanket, bread and sausage and some fruit, a bottle of cognac and two glasses. I carried ample cash and bank

The track past the Reichenbach Falls rises some 2,000 ft from Meiringen to the hamlet of Rosenlaui. Watson and I were on our way there when he was lured away to attend a sick Englishwoman, leaving me to my 'fight to the death' with Moriarty.

drafts. We could re-equip ourselves once we had reached the anonymous safety of a city on the morrow.

Seated side by side, we shared the welcome food and drink. Never, in all my days, had I envisaged the prospect of the companionship of a man whom I regarded as the epitome of human evil and had sworn to destroy. Now I was required to trust him, work with him, defend him, if it became necessary. No one save my brother Mycroft could have envisaged such an alliance; no one but he could have brought it about.

The foregoing is the true account of what happened (or, as in the case of the dog that did nothing in the night-time, did not happen) at the Falls of Reichenbach on Monday, 4 May 1891.

Watson has provided the external details in his moving narrative, *The Final Problem*: how he promptly went back up the mountain to the ledge where he had left me, and found my abandoned alpenstock where I had propped it against the rock wall, and the footprints and signs of the struggle, all of which told an obvious story to his horrified gaze. The poor fellow pathetically recounts how he even lay down in the mud, in the darkness, and shouted into the seething abyss, hearing nothing in return save the 'half-human cry of the fall'.

I was touched by the gesture when I read of it, but also relieved, for in prostrating himself there he would undoubtedly have blurred the footprints. Moriarty and I had planted them deliberately, at my instigation, but it had not been until we had been a good hour or two away from the place, and I was reviewing in my mind whether I had done everything according to plan, that it occurred to me, with a surge of self-disgust, that I had quite botched that detail. Had there been a real struggle to the death between Moriarty and me, we should scarcely have walked sedately to the point where it took place. More likely, one of us would have been backing away from the other, and therefore the two sets of prints would have been facing one another. So much for my often-reiterated insistence upon the importance of trifling details.

Perhaps, too, I ought not to have left the alpenstock leaning there; one or the other of us would surely have seized it to use as a weapon of attack or defence. However, if I had thrown it over the precipice, Watson might have concluded from its absence that I had perhaps defeated my opponent and gone on my way. In any case, I wanted the stick to draw his attention to that other clue which I had left deliberately for him to find as confirmatory evidence of what had taken place.

That object, which he could not fail to see gleaming on top of the boulder against which the alpenstock was propped, was my silver cigarette-case, containing my farewell note (written in advance in my room at the Englischer Hof):

MY DEAR WATSON –
I write these few lines through the courtesy of Mr Moriarty, who awaits my convenience for the final discussion of those questions which lie between us. He has been giving me a sketch of the methods by which he avoided the English police and kept himself informed of our movements. They certainly confirm the very high opinion which I had formed of his abilities. I am pleased to think that I shall be able to free society from any further effects of his presence, though I fear that it is at a cost which will give pain to my friends, and especially, my dear Watson, to you . . . etc.

Mycroft was pretty scathing about that note when I was at length reunited with him. The notion of Moriarty standing patiently there while I wrote it was altogether too absurd, he said, and would not have been employed by the merest hack storyteller.

'Be that as it may,' I answered, 'a note was essential, not only to let Watson see that the struggle about to commence could only have one outcome – the death of us both. Besides, I felt I owed him at least a word of farewell.

'In any case, Mycroft, you can't talk,' I added. 'Assuming that Moriarty and I had hurtled down into the Falls, there would certainly have been a search for our bodies, with every chance of finding them. They would have been almost certain to turn up in the stream below, or to be carried on by it to Lake Brienz, a few miles on. You didn't think of that, did you?'

'As a matter of fact, we did. Steiler pointed it out when we were making the arrangements. He was quite anxious about it. I considered the practicability of having substitute corpses on hand, ready to be cast adrift and be duly found. It would have involved much difficulty, and the risk of something being observed, not to mention the near-impossibility of obtaining cadavers to match a pair so distinctive as yours and the Professor's, even allowing for some unseemly mutilation. I decided to take a chance on letting it go, and Watson unwittingly helped by saying in his published account that any attempt at recovering your bodies would be hopeless.'

'You mean to say that no attempt was made, and no questions asked?'

'Oh, the police did some pretty thorough searching, of course, and there were questions at your inquest. There was nothing we dared do to try to muzzle them – that would have brought questions of a more serious nature, and given our game away. Fortunately, it was accepted that your bodies must somehow have been sucked down into whatever cauldron lies at the bottom of the waterfall. It was enough to satisfy the press, at any rate.'

'Your masters in Whitehall – that is, if you have any masters, Mycroft – must be pretty pleased with you for masterminding a coup of these proportions.'

'They will be more pleased when we can show some tangible result,' he answered seriously. 'We are not home and dry yet.'

I have been pondering this account of the sequence of events which led to my occupying the ironic position of bodyguard, companion and, it followed to some degree, assistant to the man whom history knows as my arch enemy. I have said how it came about, but not why.

The shadow of the Official Secrets Acts hangs over me; but why should it? These are personal jottings, for my amusement only, and while I suppose some public use may eventually be made of them I have certainly no intention of making them public myself. The prohibitions of the Acts are therefore immaterial, and if I do not record what actually happened during those three years of my career which I have heard referred to as the 'Great Hiatus', no one else will. The fabricated account which I gave to Watson on my reappearance in 1894 will go on being believed by the majority, while those who have always held it in some suspicion will continue to create theories and fantasies about it.

It has been asserted, for example, that I never even left London, but assumed constant disguise, in order to engage in

THE MEETING AT THE REICHENBACH FALLS

anti-criminal activities. Had I done so, I can imagine no better base for my operations than the Diogenes Club, where I could have lived under Mycroft's aegis with no one paying me enough attention to question my identity or *locus standi*. However, I did not remain in London; nor, as another theorist has suggested, did I return there after Moriarty's death at Reichenbach, in order to infiltrate a reconstituted gang, led by his military brother, whose name was also James. No such organization ever arose – or, at least, has ever been identified.

I did not go back to the United States (where at least one speculator has credited me with the unmasking, in 1892, of Lizzie Borden as the axe-murderess of her parents at Fall River, Massachusetts); nor was I in the Far East, studying the growth of Japanese militarism and her plans for the attack on China in 1894.

The most offensive of all the suggestions which have been put forward about me is that Professor Moriarty never even existed, but was an invention of mine, to enhance my reputation through Watson's chronicles; while the most ludicrous is that I am now an impostor of my previous self, having been murdered at Reichenbach by the unholy alliance of Moriarty and Watson, in satisfaction of mutual grudges against me!

None of these theories has the least degree of truth in it, and I am in need of no reassurance that I am whom I believe myself to be, and am writing this in my right mind: *Cogito, ergo sum*, in a nutshell. At the same time, I must own up, and admit that I was never in Tibet, Persia, Mecca, Khartoum, nor 'Montpelier, in the South of France', as Watson's mis-spelt version had me. I was in none of those places where I led him to believe I had been.

My period of 'Great Hiatus' was passed almost wholly in Germany, in the company of Professor James Moriarty, in the joint service of Her Majesty's Government, at the behest of my brother Mycroft.

As the world knows from his sorrowing narrative, Watson, on hastening back to the Englischer Hof, was informed by an astonished Peter Steiler that no Englishwoman, sick or well, had arrived there after our departure. He had sent no note by any boy – and a quick search for the lad himself proved in vain. Watson's account of the day's proceedings is not wholly erroneous:

> 'You did not write this?' I said, pulling the letter from my pocket.
>
> 'Certainly not,' he said. 'But it has the hotel mark upon it! Ha! it must have been written by that tall Englishman who came in after you had gone. He said – '
>
> But I waited for none of the landlord's explanations. In a tingle of fear I was already running down the village street, and making for the path which I had so lately descended. . . .

This was, to my mind, the weakest link in the whole deception of Watson. It was inevitable that he should quickly conclude who that tall Englishman must be, and recognize the trick he had played to get me alone on the mountainside; yet it would surely occur to him that in his hurried descent of the mountain track he had not passed Moriarty on his way up. I had raised this with Mycroft at the Diogenes Club, after Moriarty had gone.

'Of course I have thought of that, Sherlock,' he answered reprovingly.

'Well, then, how did Moriarty reach me without passing Watson?'

'By watching for Watson to come off the mountain, and only then hurrying up, with no need to pass him at all.'

'Knowing Watson, he'll turn straight round and dash up again, hoping to catch him before he reaches me.'

'After having already climbed up, and hurried down again – *and* with that game leg of his? No, no. He'll be far too blown.'

'He'll get the landlord to send straight round to the police. I'm sure Swiss policemen can run up mountains like goats.'

Mycroft sighed. 'Steiler, the landlord, bought his hotel with the generous bounty which Her Majesty's Government paid him for keeping us informed of the Austro-German negotiations for the Triple Alliance with Italy in '82. He is Austrian-born, not Swiss, and was our man in Vienna throughout the '70s. He is still often useful to us in Switzerland and beyond, although technically retired. You may be sure that he will contrive to delay any search of the mountain track until you and Moriarty have had ample time to get clear.'

Satisfied about that, I was able to sit back and review the scheme overall.

'It's an outlandish plan, Mycroft.'

'It is a Heaven-sent opportunity,' he corrected. 'But for friend Moriarty having been driven into a corner by your diligent operations against him, we should have had no means of enlisting his help. He would have listened to no other approach. You have achieved far more than the smashing of a criminal organization, Sherlock.'

'Assuming we can trust him.'

'That is your part of the operation – to keep him in line.' Mycroft rubbed his hands gleefully. 'The timing is immaculate. He is on the point of losing all that he has created in his years of crime. It will suit him nicely to disappear, and it will not inconvenience you.'

'There are other crimes and other criminals,' I reminded him. 'Mark my words, you will see a renewed enthusiasm among the underworld if I am believed to have left the stage for good.'

'You flatter yourself with some justice, Sherlock; but it will put Scotland Yard on their mettle to do their work without benefit of your help for a change.'

'Well, it will keep Moriarty out of mischief for a while. I doubt very much that anything will emerge from the trials that would incriminate him. He will soon be back to his old games, though. At least we know now what drove him to them.'

'Paranoia, if I'm not mistaken. He is the type who takes it for granted in any argument or contention that he must be right and his opponents wrong. The fact of his academic work being passed over would mean only one thing to him – ulterior motives, such as jealousy and spite. He could envisage no other reason. However, my inquiries lead me to believe that his work on the binomial theorem was by no means as remarkable as he would have us believe. He merely added some flourishes to what had already been adduced and published by others.'

'It won him a chair of mathematics.'

'At a *small* university. Oh, granted he has an exceptional brain – I should not have thought up this somewhat unconventional plan to make use of him, otherwise. But I would not put it past him, for example, to invent results, and dress them

up in obscure theory, in order to be seen to have reached conclusions which his instincts tell him are true, but which
he cannot prove by genuine means.'

'But *The Dynamics of an Asteroid!*' I reminded him.

'Unreviewed because it is unreviewable. It is rarefied gib-
berish. He is so convinced of his conclusion that he could not
wait to proclaim it – and because proof is called for, he pro-
vides it in a form which is incomprehensible even to the
highest minds.'

'You sound mighty sure of yourself, Mycroft. How do you
know he isn't right?'

'For all I know, he is. Some day, I shouldn't doubt, someone
will find a way of proving that that formula of his – $E = mc^2$,
isn't it? – is as correct as he believes it to be. But he cannot
prove it yet, so he invents proofs which are plausible yet
impenetrable enough to keep others from challenging them,
and risking losing face if he should happen to be right. That
is your ambitious paranoid, Sherlock – infallible in his own
eyes, and unhesitating to resort to any arrogant deceit in
order to maintain his delusion.'

'A nice companion for a disappearing trick,' I said, rising to
stretch my cramped limbs from sitting so long at the table. 'A
mad mathematician and Napoleon of Crime rolled into one.'

Mycroft, too, got up to stand facing me across the table.

'It is why I needed you, of all people, to go with him and
ensure that he carries out the task he has accepted. Naturally,
it was a foregone conclusion that he would accept it, in view
of the alternative. He claims to have done so gladly, grateful
for the chance to wipe his slate clean and atone for his past
wrongs by serving his country.'

'We have only his word for that.'

'It is a risk we have to take. He professes to be a patriot at
heart ...'

'Which could be either a straight lie, or part of his self-
delusion.'

'...The fact remains that he is the one man capable of ac-
complishing this mission, and that makes the gamble on him
worthwhile. I am hedging the bet by sending you to keep an
eye on him. Should he need help, you will provide it. On the
other hand, should he try to trick us or turn traitor, you will
be there for forestall him – even if you are forced to kill him.'

MORIARTY'S LAST CHANCE

———

OUR TASK was a straightforward one of espionage. Certain games were believed to be afoot in Germany. The British Government – or, at least, my brother Mycroft and that inner cabal whose patriotic conspiracy it was to ensure that, in matters concerning the balance of power in Europe, our country should always be the one most capable of tipping the scales to advantage – wished to know what those games were. On the face of it, it was as simple as that.

In the two or three decades before the eruption of the First World War threw almost everything into the open, unabated rivalry existed between Britain, Germany and France for influence in Europe and further afield. We were each a mighty power, rich in wealth and resources, immeasurably more advanced in the material sense than any other people in the world, with the possible exception of the United States, and enjoying profitable domination of widespread territories.

We kept open watch on Russia, and a more covert eye on one another. Did Germany lay the keel of another warship, then Britain and France regarded it their duty to have the dimensions and design of that keel in some Admiralty file, and to be kept informed, almost rivet by rivet, of the nature and progress of what came to be constructed on that foundation. Should the French add to the fortifications of Brest, or the Royal Engineers try out an air balloon, the particulars of these developments were instantly reported by the agents of all other interested parties.

Many of these agents were of the calibre of Adolph Meyer, Hugo Oberstein and Louis La Rothière, those seasoned professionals to whom my thoughts automatically flew when my aid was sought in the serious matter of the Bruce-Partington submarine plans, which I was able to recover in the nick of time before they could be auctioned among all the naval

*Gun barrels being produced at the Krupp works at Essen in Germany.
Britain, Germany and France took the keenest interest in each other's
armaments production, shipbuilding and scientific advances. I little
anticipated the day when I should find myself engaged in such espionage.*

powers of Europe. These men were well known to the authorities and their activities tolerated, so long as it remained obvious what they were doing; it was when they disappeared from sight, or appeared in unexpected places without apparent reason, that those whose responsibility it was to keep them under observation became nervous and insecure.

There were other men, and women, alien residents of the respective countries, who were in some position to supply casual information which, if evaluated as at all important, would be investigated by the professionals on the spot, or by others sent there specially.

Lowest of all in the hierarchy of espionage were those disloyal, disaffected nationals who would betray their country and their fellow natives for money or favours, or because, through dissolute or reckless behaviour, they had laid themselves open to the pressures of blackmail. These were traitors beneath contempt, and treated as such if caught.

And now there had been created another category – an unique one, comprising the unlikely teaming together of the Napoleon of Crime and – yes, I shall write it! – the foremost of all unofficial detectives. It was an uncanny experience for me: as though I were Frankenstein's monster, having had grafted on to me a controlling power of a nature alien to my own.

The train of events which had brought us to this situation had begun three years earlier in 1888, when there had appeared in a German scientific publication, *Wiedemann's Annalen* (Vol. 34), a paper entitled, in translation, *On Electromagnetic Waves in Air and their Reflection*. Its author was a thirty-one-year-old German physicist, Dr Heinrich Hertz, professor of experimental physics at the Technische Hochschule at Karlsruhe, and its content was a detailed account of how he had proved, by practical experiment, the validity of a mathematical theory which had been adduced in the previous decade by the Scottish-born physicist, James Clerk Maxwell, subsequently deceased.

Maxwell's brilliant career, in which he had sought to employ the notation of mathematics to express the electrical theories of Faraday with greater precision than could be achieved through words, had culminated in 1873 in a treatise, *Electricity and Magnetism*, which Moriarty condescended to rank almost equal with his own *The Dynamics of an Asteroid*.

'Of course,' he added bitterly, 'Maxwell kept in with *them*, in a way that I would never do. He had the chair of physics and astronomy at King's College, London, in the Sixties, but he resigned it to do his work privately on his estate in Kirkcudbrightshire. They become fidgety when one hides oneself

A cut-away view of the electrically powered submarine HOLLAND, *built by John P. Holland and accepted by the U.S. Navy in 1900. The United States and Russia were other world powers which used intensive espionage in the constant race to keep up with such developments.*

Heinrich Rudolf Hertz (1857–1894), the German physicist who, while professor of experimental physics at the Karlsruhe Polytechnic, further developed Clerk Maxwell's electromagnetic wave theories. The German government's imposition of secrecy on his work alerted our intelligence agents.

away and they can't spy on one, so they founded a professorship of experimental physics at Cambridge as bait.'

'And he took it?' I said.

'Oh, yes. Took it, and prospered. Now, I should have refused, in his place, and rejoiced at the spectacle of them thinking up new ways to lure me out.'

I forebore to point out that James Clerk Maxwell had gone on to be named among the greatest of all British physicists and mathematicians; whereas my present companion had finished up an army coach, his great talents corroded by bitterness and envy, and his academic career exchanged for one of crime –

James Clerk Maxwell (1831–1879) became one of the greatest of all British physicists and mathematicians and first professor of experimental physics at Cambridge. His ELECTRICITY AND MAGNETISM, 1873, *was rated by Moriarty almost as brilliant as his own* THE DYNAMICS OF AN ASTEROID.

in which, I might further have reminded him, he had ultimately failed, due to my personal efforts.

We had survived our night in the open air, cutting it as short as possible by arising at the first glow of dawn from behind the peaks and getting on our way. Our limbs, stiffened from the previous day's walk and the cold of the dark hours, began to respond, and we were soon making easy progress towards Lucerne. As we walked, I encouraged Moriarty to recapitulate the background to our mission. Mycroft had outlined it only sketchily to me, saying that Moriarty was fully conversant with the details.

'As I am sure you are aware,' Moriarty acceded loftily, clearly relishing his position of authority over me on this enterprise, and his superior knowledge of the facts, 'the Government employs translators whose task it is to keep up with all the foreign political, economic and scientific journals, and to draw its attention to items of likely interest. The man who read this paper of Hertz's in *Wiedemann's Annalen* passed on a précis of it to some scientific department or other in Whitehall who, in the habit of their kind, would no doubt have filed it away, had not someone of sharper than average awareness fallen to pondering the implications of Hertz's work. These are, to put it as simply as possible for your benefit...'

'*Thank* you, Professor.'

'...that if electric waves can indeed be transmitted through the air, independent of wires or cables, means might be found of manipulating and varying them, enabling them to convey messages. The army commander equipped with apparatus for receiving the transmissions, and possessing, as it were, the key to the cipher, would be able to translate them into pure language. He would no longer need to worry that his opponent might cut his telegraph wires and isolate him.'

'That is all very well so far as it goes,' I reminded him, 'but what one can do, so can another. Suppose Germany has perfected, or is trying to perfect, such a system. It is inevitable that other powers will make it their business to lay hands on the equipment and the ciphers and equip themselves to listen in at will. The wires will not have been cut; they will be laid open for all to tap.'

'That is true,' Moriarty conceded. 'But suppose that some means might be discovered of beaming the transmitted signal in a desired direction, and in no other: in effect, creating invisible wires through the air. That is going to present some problems, is it not?'

'Problems have a way of being overcome.'

'But it takes time. Whoever creates the problem holds the advantage until others catch up. That time-lag might be enough to pull off some decisive coup. Remember, Mr Holmes, that paper of Hertz's was published in '88, three years ago. Who knows how much further things have progressed and developed in that time?'

'Well, that is presumably what we are expected to find out. There is a difference between theory and practice, though.'

'Indeed. Da Vinci had the theory of man-powered flight over four hundred years ago, yet here we are in 1891, and man has yet to fly. Theory is one thing, as you say, but technical ability is another. Yet we should be gravely wanting if we were to assume that because one theory takes centuries to become reality, another one is necessarily going to. That is why I have been asked to pay this visit to Karlsruhe – to find out how they are getting on, and see whether it might not prove possible to forestall them, in our own country's interest.'

The fact that he spoke of our mission in terms of himself alone did not go unnoticed by me, yet it did not rankle. It was part and parcel of his nature that he should regard himself as the key member of our duo. Only his brainpower and training offered any hope of our being able to gain the answers we sought. When I had told my brother that I thought his scheme preposterous, he had replied: 'Sherlock, as you are aware, my respect for your talents as an investigator and deductive thinker is boundless. I am sure you would be capable of going there and insinuating yourself unsuspected among the scientific community. You would no doubt glean much knowledge, and might even penetrate to the experimental laboratories themselves. But could you interpret what you would hear and see? Come, be honest.'

My honest answer had had to be that I could not; yet I protested again at the absurdity of entrusting the work to one of the greatest criminals unhung, and a paranoiac to boot.

'For those very reasons,' Mycroft had smiled. 'Napoleon Bonaparte, for all his faults and deficiencies, achieved his best results through sheer panache. Because he believed implicitly in his personal capacity for success, he undertook enterprises which lesser men would have thought beyond them, and never even attempted. Moriarty is from the same mould. He is convinced that, in terms of intellect, he is a shark among minnows.'

'Shark indeed.'

'Granted. But at this very moment he is a deeply frustrated shark, and it is frustration which drives him most strongly. It was what impelled him to crime. When his jealous rivals denied him the fame to which he considered himself entitled,

SHERLOCK HOLMES: MY LIFE AND CRIMES

his warped mind convinced him that all men were against him, therefore he took out his revenge on society by building his criminal empire. Even in that, his academic discipline prevailed. Instead of going out and murdering a few of his detractors, he retired behind the scenes and gradually fashioned an organization capable of doing his dirty work for him.'

'It is no use being a criminal emperor if you cannot have yourself proclaimed,' I pointed out. 'And if you do that, you put a rope round your neck. He is an emperor who can never be crowned, only hanged.'

'Precisely, Sherlock! Very soon, London will ring with accounts of the uncovering of organized crime on an unprecedented scale, yet his name will not appear. He organized things so, for his security, and now, when the enormity of his evil achievement is about to be revealed, he cannot lay claim to it without incriminating himself. It has always been the one consolation of the entrapped and condemned criminal to boast the awfulness of his deeds. The speech on the scaffold, the outburst from the dock, the lurid statement to the press – Moriarty is denied any such sensational advertisement. His failure to get acclaimed for his mathematical work must seem a mere irritant compared with this. Therefore, on the eve of his Waterloo, I am offering him the chance to atone and redeem himself by doing his country a potentially great service. I put it to him that we have on our hands a problem which he alone is equipped to deal with for us – which may indeed be true. I have challenged him to prove himself. He has accepted, and I fancy it is not so much in the interest of saving his neck as of seizing what must surely be his last chance to show himself off in the role which he fancies most, the Brain of Brains.'

'Has it occurred to you, Mycroft, that your gesture might be wasted? Whatever the Germans are up to could turn out to be mere routine experimentation, of no strategic significance whatever.'

'It had, my dear Sherlock – until a report reached me recently to the effect that the German Government has taken over the direct funding of the work being done on electro-dynamics at Karlsruhe, and has forbidden publication of any further papers on the subject. That answers your question, I think?'

'Completely, my dear Mycroft.'

A Course at the

Technische Hochschule

———

After our exposed night in the mountains, Moriarty and I were thankful to reach that charming little town, Lucerne, where we took rooms in a modest but excellent pension. We were agreed that the possibility of chance recognition of either of us would be greater if we stayed at any of the more fashionable hotels.

We spent a few leisurely days re-equipping ourselves with everything appropriate to travelling gentlemen. We dined together and spent our evenings talking and playing chess, at which, needless to say, he proved exceptionally able. As our acquaintance slowly developed, there came an easing of the tension which had persisted between us ever since those moments on the ledge at Reichenbach. I confess I kept my room door locked when I retired each night, and had taken care to ascertain that there was no outside access which could have enabled Moriarty to reach my window from his. I am sure he had done the same.

The occasional jibes and sarcastic emphases which he had used in addressing me ceased. Our dealings were correct without being stiffly formal, easy without being warm, and artificially intimate and even jocular when appearances' sake called for it. I began to take a positive interest in my singular companion, studied at such close quarters.

With our personal affairs completed in Lucerne we took to the railway again, travelling to Basle, where we crossed the German border, and then to Karlsruhe, by way of Freiburg and Baden-Baden. There were, of course, no passports in those days, and my use of the name Fisher, with Moriarty calling himself Etherage, raised no problems. It was under these

The Schloss (Palace) of the Margraves of Karlsruhe, rulers of Baden,
built in 1751–1776 in the French style. Through playing in the orchestra
at a reception here I was able to see the laboratory where the secret
experiments with electromagnetic waves were being conducted.

identities that we engaged a comfortable suite of furnished
rooms in the older part of the city, whose streets fanned out
from the rather plain, eighteenth-century French-style Schloss,
built on the site of the original hunting seat of the Margrave
of Baden, Karl Wilhelm, around whom, and in whose name,
the settlement had arisen.

Having given ourselves a few days to take our bearings, we
presented ourselves at the Technische Hochschule – the Polytechnic, we should term its English equivalent now – and
were received by appointment by the Secretary, a small, fat
man, with rolls of chin and neck and a spiked moustache.

'I have your letter, Herr Etherage,' he addressed himself to
Moriarty, who looked most distinguished in his new frock
coat, winged collar, pearl pin in his tie, and with his scant
grey hair brushed back flat from his massive brow. I could see

that the oscillating movement of his head quite fascinated the other, and they put me in mind of a python swaying before a juicy prey.

'You and your friend, Herr Fisher, wish to enrol for a course of study in this establishment, I understand?'

'That is so,' Moriarty answered solemnly, countering our interviewer's heavy English with excellent German. 'My position is as follows. I have for many years been a teacher of science and mathematics at schools in England, and in recent times have been the proprietor of an establishment of my own, cramming boys for their examinations in those subjects. Mr Fisher was my chief assistant. Last year, however, I was fortunate enough to inherit a sum of money from a deceased aunt's estate, which is more than enough to assure my security for the remainder of my days.'

'If we could all live in such expectation,' murmured the Secretary, by way of a little pleasantry.

Moriarty nodded. 'I confess that the prospect of no longer having to go on trying to hammer the same things into skulls of seemingly uniform thickness comes as a boon and a relief. Mathematics had been the passion of my youth, the sustenance of my adult years. It has been my life's ambition to drink of the waters of knowledge in the country where they are most famed for their potency. To adopt musical analogy, I am like the fiddler who had once dreams of becoming a virtuoso, but had to make his career in the orchestra pit, cherishing hopelessly his ambition to study Mozart in Vienna. Where else, then, should one whose lifelong ambition it has been to indulge in mathematics seriously look than to Germany, the true home of the sciences?'

All this was clearly having its persuasive effect on the fat little official, who seemed personally flattered by it. He beamed and nodded vigorously.

'It is by no means uncommon for establishments such as this to admit amateur gentlemen.'

I did not dare glance at Moriarty's face. I doubted that even his inscrutable equanimity could have failed to be pierced by this unwitting term for the genius of the binomial theorem and the asteroid. He had no alternative to swallowing his pride, however, and could only gain a little of it back by leading the Secretary to believe that he had brought me along

109

On the left of this street in Karlsruhe stands the Technische Hochschule (Polytechnic) where the physicist Hertz investigated electromagnetic waves until the work was transferred to the secrecy of the Schloss. I was a mature student here during much of my so-called 'Great Hiatus'.

with him as a sort of paid travelling companion who would also enrol but, so his tone implied, could not hope to benefit much from the more esoteric lectures from which he himself anticipated much enlightenment.

Thus we were admitted, as fee-paying students, free to participate as diligently or sporadically as we chose in the courses of study. We had agreed to make no inquiry at this stage about the experimental work being done on the subject of electromagnetic waves. It was enough to have gained authorized entry to the Technische Hochschule's premises and spheres of activity. The rest could follow.

We were aware already that Heinrich Hertz was no longer one of the faculty. He had moved to the University of Bonn not long after the publication of his papers. This seemed at first to imply that his experimental work would have moved with him, and that the German Government's awakened interest in it had been the cause of his move. Casual inquiries revealed, though, that he was mortally ill, and had finished with experimenting; indeed, he was only thirty-seven when he died three years later, in 1894, which itself stirred my suspicions, though without justification.

Another eminent Karlsruhe experimentalist in that same sphere was Carl Ferdinand Braun, who in years to come – 1909, to be precise – would share the Nobel Prize with Marconi. He, too, had gone by the time we arrived, to assume the professorship of experimental physics at Tübingen. This seemed ominous for our hopes, but we dared ask no questions. We knew we must take our time, establishing ouselves as a couple of foreign dilettanti, while keeping our ears and eyes open. I took some delight in scoring over Moriarty by pointing out that, as the avowed mathematical enthusiast, he ought to be seen to attend assiduously, and with every show of keenness, lectures which I was certain would prove excruciatingly elementary to his advanced mind.

'You can have no conception of the tediousness of it all,' he groaned over our dinner one evening. 'It is the equivalent of Shakespeare having to listen to instruction on how to scan a metre. And when I am asked an opinion, or there is any debate, I have to make myself out a bumbling amateur and put up with their sniggering.'

'Good for the soul, Professor.'

'Pah!'

Mycroft had warned me that the European scientific community was relatively small and very 'international', as he had put it: 'Everyone knows everyone else, right across national boundaries. Our advantage with Moriarty is that while his work has been much discussed, he has remained relatively unknown as a person. But therein lies part of your task, Sherlock. Soothe him, bridle his patience. If he should lose it, through boredom or irritation, one boast from him, or a revelation of some advanced knowledge which he could not possibly possess in his pretended role would attract curiosity; and the Germans, with their thoroughness, would be sure to set inquiries afoot which we would rather were not made.'

Time passed slowly, the first year especially so. I found myself beginning to fret at the inactivity which the role of spy demanded, so different from the tension which I had expected. Our only contact with England was through Mycroft, a sparse correspondent whose letters came addressed in a variety of hands, bearing the stamps of several different countries as well as England, and obviously posted for him by his agents in those places. There seemed little likelihood that anyone in Karlsruhe held us under suspicion and would be watching our mail. Certainly we had seen nothing to alarm us, but he was clearly taking no chances.

Moriarty devoured the English newspapers, scanning each new one eagerly for details of the long drawn-out court proceedings against men and women who, I was certain, had been his unwitting hirelings. His bargain with Mycroft having included a guarantee that he would not be prosecuted, even should his involvement with any of them chance to come to light, he discussed quite openly with me those cases which he was aware that I knew were associated with him, going so far as to explain the reasons for his choice of victim, the planning, and the execution of the crimes themselves. It gave me fascinating insight into his methods. We followed the trials day by day, discussing each new facet as it emerged, and Moriarty frequently chuckled with glee at seeing how wide of the mark the prosecution sometimes fired, hampered by inexplicable gaps in the evidence.

Some of the crimes, for example, appeared quite unmotivated, especially those committed against certain academic gentlemen who, if two and two had been put together, would have been found to have been prominent in the slighting of Moriarty's publications. Disgusted as I was at the methodical way in which he had organized the financial and sexual compromise of these formerly respected people, I could not help admiring the skill with which he had found out their weaknesses and vulnerable traits, had arranged for them to be tempted, lured, and finally trapped, yet had never once shown his own hand in the business, nor given any ground for suspicion that he might be in the least involved. The list of convictions for blackmail grew, and with it the catalogue of disgrace and ruin to the victims whose real offence had been to denigrate Moriarty's scholarship. He had employed crime and the law in turn to exact his revenge. It was a veritable study in obsession, and it was painful to feel myself powerless to

112

intervene and help save those wretched victims from the worst effects of their downfall.

My mind inevitably looked to the day when our mission should be at an end. What would become of this monster then? Would our success – assuming that we achieved it – be enough to reform him, or at least persuade him that, his lust for vengeance sated, he had no reason for returning to a career of crime? I went so far as to question whether it might not eventually be my duty to give him the silver bullet or drive the stake through his heart, and so settle the question.

Come to that, what plans might he have concocted for me in some of his more darkly brooding moments? Having revealed so much of himself to me, he could scarcely afford to let me live to hound him again, once our enforced armistice was over.

Something else puzzled me in a less abstract way. Watching him scan each newspaper report, it seemed to me that he was expecting to find something which consistently failed to appear. It could scarcely be his own name. The bulk of the proceedings was over, without one mention of him – and, even had it appeared, it would have been as the *late* Professor Moriarty.

It was not that; yet I could sense an aura of apprehension growing about him. Obliquely I tried to draw him out about it. He did not respond; but I could tell that he was becoming a worried man – and that in turn worried me.

A MOST INGENIOUS GUN

IT WOULD have been expecting too much of the Polytechnic authorities that they should find it plausible for an English amateur and his friend to apply themselves constantly and indefinitely to a study of mathematics, even out of professed pleasure. Moriarty and I therefore made quite frequent trips away from Karlsruhe.

Like myself, he was a musical enthusiast, and we conceived the agreeable idea of travelling in the steps of the Mozart family, passing time in such south German and Rhineland cities as Munich, Augsburg, Mainz, Frankfurt, Coblenz and, of course, Mannheim, which was no distance from Karlsruhe. At another time we visited Salzburg, Vienna and Linz. Moriarty was at pains to stress the genius Mozart's aptitude for mathematics which, next to music, was his keenest interest. I believe he was attempting to adduce that mathematics and the utmost refinement of mind were inseparable companions; he pointed also to the Goldberg Variations of Bach as a mathematical exercise *par excellence*. I retorted amiably that Beethoven had been little more than competent to count the change in his pocket, yet had managed pretty well in the musical line with the assistance of the sounds and sights of Nature; and that the Diabelli Variations, in their different way, were quite as remarkable as the Goldberg.

It was at this period that my attention was drawn to the works of Orlandus Lassus who, with Palestrina, shared the very peak of European musical composition in the sixteenth century. He had been born in Belgium, but spent most of his adult life in Munich, where he died in 1594. Descendants of his lived there still, and our first visit coincided with the sale by them of some of his papers and the publication of a slim volume of his letters, with commentaries. I attended the sale and bought a number of items, and also acquired the book and one

114

or two others on the subject of this remarkable man who had composed well over two thousand works, among them no less than five hundred motets.

The discovery could not have come at a better time. It was becoming ever more obvious to me that our assignment, already more than a year old, was destined to last much longer. My preconceptions of the spy's trade had already been much revised. In combating crime, I was accustomed to working retrospectively, so to speak. The crime came first, almost invariably unforeseen, and my function was to piece together the circumstances and any clues and inescapable inferences, and deduce the chain of events which had led up to it. Only

A 1582 edition of some motets by the German composer Orlandus Lassus (his name is rendered in differing ways). My study of his works during my Karlsruhe period culminated in the publication in 1896 of my monograph ON THE POLYPHONIC MOTETS OF LASSUS.

SHERLOCK HOLMES: MY LIFE AND CRIMES

then could I begin to determine precisely how the crime had been committed, and the physical and perhaps mental characteristics of the unknown person responsible. From there I could reach certain conclusions and cast my thoughts forward, to forecast his or her subsequent actions and their implications, and work out where he would most likely be found, and how best tackled.

The whole process seldom took more than a few days for, as I have always preached, reasoning backwards offers no difficulties. People habitually tend to look forward, to what they believe or imagine is likely to become of them should this or that course of action be followed; indeed, that is the essential process for dealing with the everyday affairs of life. Yet my art, which impressed people as so sensational, was the relatively simpler one. After all, it was based on the consideration of known facts, whereas to speculate forward is to deal with the unknown. This has always been to me one of the most obvious facts of life, yet I stand by my wager that for every fifty persons who base their reasoning on uncertainties, only one troubles to analyse what has passed, and base his reasoning on that. It is a truism that the deeper one's knowledge of history, the better one can understand one's present fellow men; and in no field does that apply more than in the solution of crimes. Countless results of mine have been achieved by the study of precedents.

Espionage, on the other hand, I found to be a very different business. It is wholly forward-looking: a question of finding out others' circumstances and intentions; not what they have done, but what they might do, and when, and how, and with what undisclosed advantages. It is a slow, painstaking process of listening, watching and waiting, often for scant results or even none at all, and therefore as ill-suited as any career could be to a man of my temperament.

Hence my delight in the discovery of Lassus and his music, which was as little performed and regarded at the time of which I am writing as Purcell or Monteverdi. Mendelssohn, Brahms, Liszt and Saint-Saëns were the admired ones then: the Tudor school and their foreign contemporaries were seldom heard. Through Richter, Sarasate, Madame Norman-Neruda and other admired executants I had sated myself with the melodious and easily accessible music of the nineteenth century. Our long and largely inactive Karlsruhe vigil caused my mind to call out for some stimulus, some intellectual quest which might absorb me and keep my brain exercised.

That was how I came to compose my monograph *On the Polyphonic Motets of Lassus*, which those few experts who commented on it were kind enough to agree constituted the last word upon the subject. It was published in 1896 in a small, limited edition, which I did not take the trouble to enter at Stationers' Hall or give to the national collections. Martha and I have hunted everywhere for my own sole copy of it, but in vain. Surviving copies must be few and far between, and I dare say little consulted, for Lassus and his contemporaries remain beyond the perception of most music lovers.

The challenge of studying those more than five hundred complex works of vocal counterpoint, however, was undertaken less as a contribution to musical scholarship than to occupy a restless mind. Watson, seeing me at work on the latter stages of this research, in the year before the monograph's publication, imagined with characteristic naivety that it was a recently acquired 'hobby'. It was nothing of the sort, having occupied me during several years by then, and one scarcely 'takes up' an esoteric interest, in the sense of deciding to collect stamps or cigar bands. But I gave up concerning myself over Watson's musical preferences long since. How can one hope to impress a musical taste with aspirations no higher than the music hall and Gilbert and Sullivan?

I had, incidentally, hoped to discover that Lassus had preceded me in the spying trade. It was quite the thing in his day for musicians, poets, priests and others with privileged entry to foreign courts; and I suspect that, whenever he returned to Munich, the Emperor Maximilian would have summoned his distinguished servant to the Presence, to deliver up an account of all that he had seen and heard. I found nothing substantial enough to work upon, however.

Besides, I had business of that sort of my own to demand my attention, as I was reminded during a further visit to Munich with Moriarty. My purpose was to seek out any of those Lassus descendants, in the hope that there might exist family records hitherto undisclosed. It was Moriarty, however, who had proposed the visit, speaking vaguely of business which he wished to attend to there. I knew that the ill-gotten gains from his criminal career were spread among many banks in a number of countries, and no doubt one of them was in Munich.

The agitation which I had noticed in him had been increasing lately. I had been inclined to put it down to that same sense of dissatisfaction which lack of positive action had engendered in me; but I was more than a little surprised when, walking along a narrow street in the neighbourhood of our unremarkable hotel, on the way back from a library, I saw that unmistakable form loom forth from a narrow doorway some way ahead of me, and make briskly off in the hotel's direction. There was no mistaking the tall, rather stooped figure, the somewhat splay-footed gait, or – most telling of all – the unceasing oscillation of the head. I had the impression that he was trying to appear rather less than usually conspicuous by turning up his coat's astrakhan collar about his ears, and withdrawing his head into it like a tortoise's into its shell.

He did not see me, and I did not hail him, or try to catch up. Instead, I crossed the road to get a comprehensive view of the premises he had just quit, without having to stop outside and crane my neck to read the inscription over the window, which was close shuttered. In unobtrusively small German script it read: *A. von Herder: Mechanical Instruments.*

Here was a slight puzzle which I decided to waste no time in solving. Crossing the road again, I opened the shop door and stepped briskly in.

It was not so much a shop, as a workshop, with only a small counter for the ledgers. The rest of the space was occupied by lathes, work-benches, and small machines, operated by belts driven by overhead wheels. There was a pervading smell of metal and oil.

The only person there was a small elderly man with white hair, his clothing protected by a grease-stained canvas overall. The only striking feature about him was his eyes: they were completely opaque, the pupils covered over with a bluey white film. I saw at once that he was totally blind. The metal object which he was holding was a rifle barrel.

In German, I introduced myself by the name Jakob Mauerstein, and said that I was anxious to purchase a revolver, and had been recommended to him by a colleague. When he asked the colleague's name I answered that I knew him only as Schmidt, which provoked a knowing smile.

'What manner of revolver are you seeking, Herr Mauerstein?' he asked.

'Nothing large and clumsy. Something . . . discreet. Capable, say, of being carried in a jacket pocket without causing an unsightly bulge.'

Despite the blankening effect of his blindness on his expression, he appeared puzzled.

'The calibre could not be high, and there would be other limitations.'

'That is quite understandable.'

'Then, if I am not mistaken, sir, you require merely a standard weapon, without special refinement?'

'That is so.'

'Oh, then I'm afraid your friend Herr Schmidt has misinformed you. I carry no stock of that nature. Everything is made specially to order, to meet the customer's particular requirements. What you want would be readily obtainable from any gunsmith in the city.'

I made a little sound of irritation. 'I apologize for wasting your time, Herr von Herder. I shall give Schmidt a good ticking-off. He should have known better.'

The old man had taken no offence, and we exchanged courtesies before I took my leave, with the name and address of a conventional gunsmith whom he recommended.

I did not go there, however. The visit to von Herder's had told me all I needed to know. He made only special weapons, of a kind evidently unobtainable across the counter. And the last customer to place an order, and write his name and address in the blind mechanic's ledger, and against it the not inconsiderable amount he had paid by way of deposit, was one Etherage, with an address which was extremely familiar to me in Karlsruhe.

THE REPULSIVE RUSSIAN

NATURALLY, IT was my habit to search Moriarty's room from time to time, and I knew, from the way my little traps were sprung, that he returned the compliment. We expected it of one another, and never referred to it, let alone objected.

For some weeks following our return to Karlsruhe from the latest visit to Munich I made a point of not carrying out any such routine inspection. I was content to wait; and, sure enough, in about two months' time he remarked casually that he had further business in Munich. I was sure that I pleased him by saying I did not fancy a trip myself just at the moment, and left him to go alone.

'Everything satisfactory, Professor?' I greeted him cheerfully upon his return.

'Thank you, Mr Holmes.'

'My word, that's a handsome new cane you've treated yourself to!'

He grimaced. 'For the first time in my life, I left my old faithful in a cab. I inquired at the rank, but it had not been reported found. One can never trust those fellows.'

'Well, you've done yourself proud. Solid silver head?'

'Yes, yes. Perhaps a trifle extravagant, but ...'

He shrugged, and left me, without proffering the new cane for me to examine. I had spared him the embarrassment, for there was no need. Silver top notwithstanding, I knew perfectly well how expensive it must have been, and how deceptively light it would feel for a rifle in disguise. The blind man of Munich was undoubtedly a consummate craftsman. All that would be needed was a twist and pull upon that silver head, and the firing mechanism would emerge and a skeleton grip automatically unfold.

What I could not fathom was why Moriarty had decided to arm himself. On Mycroft's express orders we had brought no weapons to Germany. We were being sent to gather information, not to indulge in violent adventures, he had lectured us sternly, and going about unarmed would help keep us out of temptation. Besides, if we did become suspect and our things were searched, the finding of arms would not aid us to profess our innocence convincingly. He had, of course, added the superfluous warning that should we find ourselves accused of spying, the British government would deny any connection with us and do nothing to help us.

Yet now Moriarty had acquired this expensive weapon, which he could carry openly yet unsuspected wherever he went, and use in a flash, for I had no doubt that it was ready-loaded. But why? At least I felt pretty certain that it was not for use against me. If he wished to kill me he could do so whenever he chose, for we were almost constantly together, by ourselves or in company.

I hoped he had not entered into some ploy of his own to get hold of the information we were seeking, and was anticipating some risks. I wanted him neither harmed, nor skipping off with secrets in his pocket for delivery to some other power with whom he had joined in a double-crossing conspiracy. The intimacy and mutual understanding which we had established by being thrown so much together could turn out to be a huge bluff on his part; indeed, it occurred to me that the increasing signs of tension which I had noticed in him might be due to his winding himself up for action. I resolved to watch him ever more keenly, taking particular note of anyone with whom he had dealings, however innocent-seeming. Apart from anything else, if he did propose to defect, he might decide to kill me as a form of bonus. It behoved me to be extra alert.

Meanwhile, things continued as usual. Although we had kept much to ourselves when not attending lectures, we had made a point of fraternizing with fellow students in the coffee houses and beer halls which were virtually extra-curricular departments of the Technische Hochschule. Good conversation was to be had, chess and draughts were played, lusty German songs were bellowed with much rhythmic thumping of beer steins, and the beer or coffee went down in companionable style. Sometimes I obliged with accompaniments or solos on a borrowed fiddle, and received warm compliments on my playing.

121

A Bier-keller of the kind much patronized by German students.
I spent many hours in such establishments in Karlsruhe, joining in
the rumbustious choruses and sometimes entertaining with my violin,
as a result of which I was enabled to locate the secret laboratory.

The students were by no means all youngsters, though youth did predominate. Not a few were mature dilettanti like ourselves. We were the only Englishmen, but there were a good many other non-Germans. One of these, I learned years later, was a fellow spy; or perhaps it would be truer to say that he shortly became one. His presence among us, personally repellent though we found him, proved a happy coincidence for Moriarty and me.

He was Ievno Azeff, a Russian Jew in his early twenties. It was not that which offended us, but his appearance – he was short, stout and hirsute, with dirty fingernails, and clothing which neither looked nor smelled clean – and his personal habits, and his coarse conversation. When holding forth, his chief topic was his irresistible appeal to women, the results of which he delighted in describing in the lewdest terms.

Because we were English, and therefore certain to be prudish, he took some pleasure in addressing himself directly to us. We remained stony-faced, and I imagine Moriarty's grim oscillations finally unnerved him, for he ultimately found occasion to come across and call for drinks for us, and tried to get us to chat. Inevitably, though, the subject soon turned round to himself.

'You know why I come here? I'm at home in Rostov. Rostov on the Don, huh? Well, I get hard up, so I steal money from an old guy, huh? What hell it matter to him – he got plenty. I got none. I steal.'

He broke off into a peal of raucous laughter.

'So, cops come looking for me, and I'm getting out of Rostov dam' quick, hey? Then I'm wand'rin' around Poland, and into Germany. And then finding this nice big girl in Berlin . . . Aw, I tell you last night – how her husband come in, remember?'

He rocked with amusement again.

'So I'm out of Berlin dam' fast, too, and a train lands me up in this place. And I'm seeing Polytechnic, and I'm thinking, "Hey, Ievno, you gotter lie up somewhere a little bit. Maybe this place do." So I'm enrolling for a course here in electric engineering.'

If Moriarty experienced the same stab of excitement as I, he concealed it masterfully. Our repulsive little companion had given us the lead for which we had been waiting patiently for so long.

123

' Take another drink?' I suggested.

'Sure. Make it schnapps. This beer gives me gas.'

He eructated uninhibitedly. I caught Moriarty's passing eye. It was as expressionless as ever, but I knew that our opportunity had been presented to us, and any vulgarity could be tolerated towards that end.

In all our time in Karlsruhe we had never broached the subject of the experimental work in electromagnetics which had brought us here. We wished to be known as amateurs of mathematics, nothing more – a pair of mildly eccentric, unworldly, trusting and trustful Englishmen: living equivalents of the types frequently depicted in cartoon drawings in the more bellicose German newspapers and magazines. Considering that Karl Marx and Friedrich Engels were able to practise their insidious activities in England in the 1850s and, upon investigation, be passed over as odd, but harmless, we fancied our chances of remaining undetected were good. A false or impatient move, however, might attract unwanted attention. The Germans, with no girdle of sea surrounding their frontiers, are apt to be less insular and complacent than we British.

Our time together, and our many discussions about our task, had pretty well attuned Moriarty and me to one another's processes of thought. Our unspoken, mutual opinion regarding Azeff was that it was an odd thing for a criminal on the run to do – to sign on for a polytechnic course in a foreign land. A more likely possibility was that he was on the same quest as we, and was doing a little fishing, to find out whether we were what we seemed. Or he might be an *agent provocateur* for the Germans, who had decided that the time had come to put us to the test.

'Is it an interesting course?' I inquired mildly.

'Huh? Aw, yeh, I guess so. I did a couple year in Rostov before I get into trouble. I guess a man need to qualify in something to keep him, till rich old widow give him eye. Know what I mean?'

'Yes, I see. How long do you expect to stay on here?'

He shrugged. 'While money last out – or widow show up.'

In more secure circumstances it would have been our chance to offer to replenish his funds in exchange for information. It was more than we dared. I risked lingering on the subject for a little longer, though.

'Didn't I hear that this is a pretty notable place for research in your field? A Professor Hart... Hurth...?'

'Hertz. He move on some place.'

'And took his research with him?'

'Aw, no. Is going on still. They make it secret, though, and take it up to Schloss. Hey!' His face brightened again. 'Mebbe that what I do. I write to Ochrana and say I make report if they are letting me come home and giving me plenty roubles. Hey, Herr *Wirt*! Schnapps and beer.'

'You had better take care, making jokes like that in public,' said Moriarty gravely. 'The German sense of humour has its limitations.'

'Huh? Aw, I get it. Mebbe not making joke, though.'

He tapped the side of his nose and leered horribly.

Suddenly, I pretended to take him seriously, and with awe. 'You mean, you'd break into the castle somehow and steal the secrets for the Russian secret service?'

'Why not? Plenty roubles. Maybe rich and *young* widow then.' He indulged briefly in a further bout of spluttering laughter. 'You British, you taking all serious. You think I tell you if I make real plan, huh?'

I affected relief. 'I knew you were pulling our legs.'

'Aw, no. I see way you look. Ievno Azeff pretty dam' smart guy. Listen me – if Ochrana saying "Okay, Ievno, you get dam' plans, we give you roubles," you bet I get.'

'From... from up there in the castle?' I strove my hardest to sound aghast. 'But it must be heavily guarded. I mean to say, if you're right in thinking the research laboratory has been moved there...'

Our companion growled and tossed down his schnapps.

'Ievno want, Ievno get. Is so always.'

He got up impatiently and went to join some others.

'This is most frustrating, Mr Holmes,' Moriarty murmured. 'Had he been an Englishman, I should have been tempted to enlist his services here and now.'

I agreed, adding, 'I'm inclined to think he is precisely what he makes himself out to be – a dare-devil who is game to risk anything for a good enough reward. But it could be fatal to confide in him. At the very least, he would probably contrive to blackmail us. At the worst, he would lead us on, compromise us thoroughly, then sell us out.'

'Then we make no use of him. That is not to say that we discard what he has told us as well.'

'Get into the Schloss ourselves? I quite agree.'

'The only question is how – short of getting ourselves invited to one of the Margrave's receptions. I don't see two obscure foreigners achieving that very easily.'

I did not, either. But his words had given me an idea. I proposed that we take our leave of the beer-cellar, and that I would tell him an idea in surroundings where we would be safe from being overheard. Moriarty agreed, and took up his lethal stick, and we sauntered out into the fresh air.

I am looking at a photograph of Ievno Azeff which I came across in later years. He is a few years older than when I met him, but maturity had not improved his looks.

He left Karlsruhe a few weeks after our conversation, which does indeed seem to have sparked the decision which was to launch him upon his notorious career as ruthless *agent provocateur* and spy for the Tsarist secret police, the Ochrana. He did write to them, apparently, offering his services and was engaged at fifty roubles a month (not quite up to his boasted expectations, I fancy) to infiltrate the revolutionary societies of expatriate Russians in Germany. His misdemeanours in his native Russia were evidently forgiven, for he was next engaged in spying on underground revolutionary organizations in Moscow itself.

He went on to higher – or, as I should say, lower – things by planning and carrying out the assassination of the Tsar's uncle, the Grand Duke Sergius. Another important victim of his was Plehve, the unpopular Minister of the Interior who was politically responsible for the Ochrana itself, and whom Azeff was supposed to be protecting.

Circumstances forced him to escape to Germany again. Someone who met him in Frankfurt in 1912 described him as bitter at having been cheated of his lifelong ambition, which was to assassinate the Tsar.

What his own fate was I never heard. The photograph shows him sea-bathing somewhere, in the company of a tall, somewhat buxom, and not unattractive young woman, whom he is holding by the hand with every appearance of satisfaction. Perhaps Ievno got what Ievno wanted, after all, and, like many other notorious men, died in connubial bliss.

126

The Russian spy and AGENT PROVOCATEUR *Ievno Azeff was at the beginning of his infamous career when he was a fellow student of mine at Karlsruhe Polytechnic. Despite his appearance and personal habits, he boasted many conquests among the opposite sex.*

A MUSICAL EVENING

'HIGHLY INGENIOUS, Mr Holmes. But you have overlooked a detail of some importance to me.'

'What is that, Professor?'

'If you go alone, you will not know what to look for. And even should you come upon it by chance, you will not recognize it. Dear me, your self-assurance is almost as inflated as that abominable Russian's.'

'Very well,' I retorted. 'You go instead; but you had better commence fiddle lessons without delay.'

I had outlined my plan to gain admittance to the Schloss, which formed the focal point of the city. Karlsruhe, like most German cities and towns of any size, had its own theatre and theatre orchestra, and it had also a conservatoire of music; but it was by no means a centre of music and culture. The old custom of state rulers to maintain their court orchestras had ceased to flourish. The nature of music and the make-up of the orchestra itself had changed much in the latter half of the century, and public performances of a high standard were well established. The princes and dukes and archbishops were happy to be spared the expense of retaining court musicians, and when they gave a reception or a ball they were more likely to turn to the military: the continental military bands of the time were more like orchestras, with strings and other instruments out of place on a British bandstand.

Entertainments at the Schloss were not frequent and were strictly by invitation, generally in connection with a visit from some other dignitary who needed to be impressed with a show of culture, or at least given some music to dance to. The Margrave's officials recruited for each occasion from among freelance musicians in the city who, in lieu of being paid a retainer, were given a concert fee with the concession that, should they be unable to take up an engagement, they could put in a deputy, rather than relinquish the offer. The deputy got whatever portion of the fee his hirer chose to pay him.

My violin playing in the cafés and taverns had brought me the acquaintance of several musicians with whom I had shared many a pleasant hour of chat and drink – the latter tending to be their priority. More than once it had been remarked that I was good enough for the Margrave's orchestra, and one congenial fellow of whom I had made an especial friend had flippantly promised to let me deputize for him if ever I chose to. He was ardently courting a pretty sweetheart to whom he devoted every available hour, but did not wish to sever his court connection. I knew that I had only to drop the word to him that I should be willing to play as his deputy when the occasion next arose. He would be certain to accede.

This was what I suggested to Moriarty, following our chat with Azeff. Musical though he was, he was no musician, so there was no question of taking him with me. His sour response to the idea was, I guessed, because he disliked the prospect of my being able to penetrate where he could not. It exacerbated that derangement which made him suspect that anything he could not see or share might prove detrimental to him.

I explained the position in the most reassuring words I could find. It was necessary to get into the Schloss, where we now knew the secret laboratory to be. I had a legitimate reason for admission which he had not. All I proposed to do was locate the laboratory and ascertain what it would take to gain re-entry for the pair of us.

'I could come with you,' he argued. 'I could at least carry an instrument and look like a musician.'

'Too many of the other players know us both. They know you don't play. Attention would be bound to be drawn to you, and questions asked.'

'If you are alone, how do you expect to go hunting about the place? You will be sitting on your stool, fiddling.'

'There are the intervals. Quite long ones. Even musicians get some supper and need to use lavatories. I shall make my opportunities, never fear.'

'It will be like looking for a needle in a haystack.'

'Great heavens, it isn't the Tower of London. It is a small Schloss. I could almost guess from here where a laboratory would be located.'

'Where?'

'As high up as possible. The top floor or even a special construction on the roof.'

'What leads you to that belief?'

'They are experimenting with transmitting electrical waves through the atmosphere. It stands to reason that they will have selected a place where there is as little natural obstruction to the path of the waves as possible.'

'Well, even supposing you know what to look for you will never get into the laboratory. It is certain to be guarded.'

'Professor Moriarty,' I said, 'if, in pursuing your criminal enterprises, you had taken more part in the action, and not delegated it all to others in order to maintain your anonymity and invisibility, you would not be wasting words on such trifling considerations. You are like one of those generals who leads his regiment from behind. He may get his results, but it is through the efforts of others. You are a strategist by nature. I am a tactician.'

'Stop, stop! Dear me, Mr Holmes, dear me, you are becoming quite heated. I was merely testing all the possibilities, as I think you would agree a good general should.'

I could have smiled. By a chance analogy, I had restored his sense of his importance, enabling him to see himself in the light of a commander sending forth his reconnoitring minions, like Joshua before Jericho: 'Go, view the land, even Jericho'. I could only hope that, when the time came, the Germans were not as quick as the King of Jericho's counter-agents at spotting a spy.

At any rate, we now had a plan. Moriarty's pride was satisfied and he was happy to give his assent. All I needed was to hear of a summons to the musicians; and even that proved not long in coming. I 'chanced' to meet my violinist friend and offered my services. He was overjoyed, the more so when I waved aside his embarrassed proposal regarding the fee, which was small enough, anyway.

'I must not sully my amateur status,' said I. 'The experience, and the privilege of viewing the Schloss from within, are all that I could ask.'

And so, attired in my evening things, I joined the party of musicians at their usual meeting place on the evening of the concert and made my way up to the castle with them. My preoccupation with the motets of Orlandus Lassus was known to most of them, and there was a good deal of chaff about the possibility of my serious mind rebelling against the works of the Strauss family, Offenbach, Millöcker, Zeller, Suppé, and other composers of the operetta music which would comprise the evening's entertainment. In fact, I admired, as I have never ceased to do, the best works of such men. Music does not deserve to be sneered at as 'cheap' simply because it is popular and has no appeal to intellectual snobbery. Strauss and Offenbach are as worthy and admirable in their way as Lassus and Palestrina in theirs.

The castle official whose function it was to assemble the orchestra greeted my companions and welcomed me courteously when they introduced me. I told him that I deemed it an honour to be invited to play in privileged surroundings, to which he replied that it was a pleasure to welcome an Englishman to the castle.

'This happens to be the first time I have ever set foot in a Schloss,' I told him. 'One admires them from afar as features of a landscape that is so different from our own, but the only impression one has of them inside is from photographs.'

I glanced about the lobby where we were assembled. It was nothing exceptional, architecturally or decoratively, and rather gaudy, I felt, with its pillars and arches and many-coloured friezes and borders; but I murmured, 'Magnificent! Remarkable!'

It had the effect I desired. 'Herr Fisher,' he said, 'you will permit me to escort you on a general tour during one of the interludes?'

'Oh, but that would be expecting too much. You must have so many other things to do.'

'Not at all. Your colleagues are well familiar with the routine of these occasions and need no looking after. I will seek you out at a convenient point in the evening.'

He bowed and went away. A conducted tour would scarcely include the one room which really interested me in the place, but it would eliminate a good many of the others and narrow down any search I was able to make on my own account; and the use of elimination to lead me to that which I was seeking had always stood high in my list of the essential principles of deduction.

131

Dancing at a reception similar to that at which I played in the Margrave of Karlsruhe's orchestra. Although the light dance music was in total contrast with my austere classical preferences, I found much to admire in the compositions of the Strauss family and others of their ilk.

The ballroom in which we played on a permanent dais at one end was much as I had expected, with the same gaudy trappings, involving the collision of primary colours, and gilt on anything offering itself to be gilded. The Margrave and his family made an undistinguished, if garish group. Military uniforms of blue and green and red, with much gold lace, contrasted with the colours of ladies' gowns and the black frock coats of the male civilians. But when we struck up our music the dancing got off to an enthusiastic start, stiffness gave way to smiles, and general enjoyment prevailed. I found no problems with the music, playing by sight the catchy pieces, some of which I had never even heard before, let alone tried, and found myself quite absorbed by the sometimes intricate skill with which the composers of this lighter type of music achieved their felicitous effects. From the safety of the second violins I could do no harm by my mistakes, and flattered myself that I made no more of them than any of the others.

The tempo was for the most part brisk, with polkas much in demand, so that there were plenty of pauses for both dancers and musicians to get back their breath. As the evening progressed, the interludes became longer, to give leisure for refreshments. I enjoyed an excellent supper, with liberal champagne.

At length the usher sought me out. I thought that he had not been stinting himself either.

'Bring your glass,' he said, draining his full one at a single swallow. He gestured to one of the footmen to open another bottle of champagne and hand it over.

'Come,' said my friend to me. 'No point in going thirsty whilst I show you about.' Carrying the bottle by its neck in one white-gloved hand, and his glass in the other, he led the way from the supper room and up the broad sweep of the main staircase leading from the lobby.

Our progress took us through a succession of rooms typical of a rather grand country mansion: drawing-rooms of various sizes, a music room, a library, furnished as such apartments are apt to be, more for effect than for domestic comfort. He gave me a peep into the Margrave's study, and into the bedrooms on the floor above. Another staircase led further up. We paused at its foot, while he replenished our glasses yet another time and we drank.

'Servants' quarters, mostly,' he gestured to the stairs. He seemed to hesitate for a moment, and then said, 'They tell me you're taking mathematics at the Polytechnic.'

I laughed dismissively. 'Hardly. I came over here with my old headmaster – I was an assistant teacher of his. He came into money and retired, and since mathematics had always been his hobby, and he'd heard of the courses here, he enrolled and persuaded me to come for company.'

'Boring sort of way to pass the time, what?'

'Oh, I don't do much work. I leave that to old Etherage – my boss. I've been to some of the lectures to try to improve my mind, you know, but mathematics would never be my subject in this world.'

'What was your subject as a teacher?'

'History – though in our private schools one's expected to turn one's hand to almost anything. Barring maths, chemistry and physics, I must have run the gamut in my day. I draw the line at those, though. They're completely beyond my comprehension.'

'Have another glass.'

'Thanks.'

'How long are you and Herr . . . Etherage . . . proposing to stay here?'

'It's up to him. I'd go home and leave him to it, only he begs me to stay, and he makes it worth my while. He says he couldn't fancy being a lone Englishman here.'

'If he, too, would be interested to see around the Schloss, by all means make an appointment with me and I shall be happy to conduct you again. Any time. There is no need to wait for another reception.'

'That's most kind of you. The old boy hasn't much sense of history or art or anything, but I'm sure he'd feel it a privilege to look round.'

To my surprise, the official started up the staircase.

'There's something up here which might interest him more,' he said over his shoulder, and my heart thumped suddenly, not simply from the effort of climbing the rather steep stairs.

We reached a long, narrow landing, with many doors to what I supposed were the servants' rooms. There were yet more stairs to climb, and then another similar corridor. Considering the number of servants in evidence down below it was not surprising that so much of the castle was given over to accommodating them.

'Only one more to go,' said my friend, and refreshed us both for the ascent from the now almost empty bottle.

The last staircase led to a shorter landing with fewer doors. We passed along towards the one at the very end. It bore the inscription, in old German script *Eingang Verboten!*

My friend winked at me and produced a bunch of keys.

'No entry, as you see, so don't tell anyone I showed you in.'

134

'Of . . . of course not. What is it?'

He reached in for an electric light switch. We were standing in a rather bare, plain room. It could only be the laboratory which was the object of my search, but it resembled no other laboratory of my experience.

It was some fifteen metres long and only a little less broad. It contained almost nothing in the way of furniture: a plank table, some bench seats and a platform arrangement. There were no retorts, test tubes, bottles of liquids and powders; nothing resembling the customary laboratory equipment. Instead, there were metallic devices: square plates of what looked like zinc, with brass rods protruding from them which terminated in small brass balls, polished to exceeding brightness; copper coils, with wires trailing from them; Leyden jars, with copper coatings over half their surface and copper wires connecting these outer coatings with something inside; brass cylinders, and large parabolic metal shapes which I decided must be reflectors.

All this I took in as I traversed the room with my eyes, striving to impress on my mind any detail which might be informative to Moriarty. There were no blackboards bearing chalked formulae, no notes lying about.

The thought flashed into my mind that the Germans might have come to suspect our purpose in Karlsruhe. I had been deliberately brought to this room of secrets, where my guide would in a moment reveal himself to be a willing traitor to his country. He had shown me that it existed, and would proceed to offer up its secrets at a later time, in return for the fortune which we should meanwhile have persuaded our government to remit to him. If I were crass enough to entertain his proposal for one moment he would have the confirmation he needed as to Moriarty's and my purpose there.

Such was my thought; it occupied perhaps a fraction of a moment to conceive, and was followed by as prompt a resolution to maintain my innocent pose and simply hope that I could yet find some means of getting Moriarty into this place for a detailed examination.

It was my last thought, before a heavy blow on the back of my skull sent me staggering to the floor; and as the floorboards seemed to rush up to meet me all consciousness faded into blackness and oblivion.

POLICE HEADQUARTERS

THE OFFICE of the Chief of Police was as drab and grey as the stone-faced building which housed it. The official himself matched his surroundings: a light grey suit, grey spats over his black shoes, a drawn, parchment-hued face, and once-black hair fading away to grey and silver.

Moriarty and I occupied chairs before his large desk. To one side sat the plump little Secretary of the Technische Hochschule and, at the other end of the desk, the usher who had escorted me on the tour of the Schloss, whose lasting impression on me was a tender and aching head. Two uniformed policemen stood behind us, guarding the door, and another was seated at a distance, taking notes on a pad.

The Chief removed his silver *pince-nez* and massaged the bridge of his long nose, where the spring had marked it.

'I suppose you have some sort of story trumped up,' he said in toneless German. 'We might as well get it over with.'

'I have a great deal to say,' I answered warmly.

'Then proceed, Herr Fisher. It will all be taken down.'

It was early in the morning following my experience. I had regained consciousness to find myself sprawled on the laboratory floor, about to be lifted up by uniformed flunkeys. My guide was looking on with a dispassionate expression. I could recollect everything that had happened, even to the impact of the blow on my skull.

'What . . . happened?' I had asked, striving to maintain my innocent role. 'Did I faint? The . . . the champagne?'

No answer came. I was carried without undue effort at gentleness down the successive flights of narrow stairs, then through a door in one of the lower corridors, leading on to further stairs. At length a heavier door was unbolted and I was borne into the cold night air, for whose refreshing impact I was thankful. The dark form of a carriage and horses loomed.

A policeman was holding open the door. I was bundled in, and found another uniformed policeman already there. His companion joined us, the door slammed to, and a muffled order set the horses into motion.

I kept asking what had happened to me, and where we were going, and what about my coat and my violin – anything which I judged a harmless foreigner who has just met with some bewildering accident would seek to know. My escorts might as well have been deaf mutes, for all the response they made.

After some ten minutes' fast travelling the coach pulled up and I was thrust out, made to use my own legs this time, but with a tight grip on each of my arms to support and restrain me. I was bustled up steps, along a passage and past some desks, where seated policemen stared curiously at my passing; then down more steps – stone, this time – and into a narrow, unlighted cell. A metal door clanged to behind me.

It had all been done with scarcely a word uttered, except by me. I did not even know how long I had been unconscious. My guess, however, was that a blow on the head from an empty champagne bottle – which was the one detail I took for granted – would not have laid me out for more than a matter of minutes. The rest had happened with remarkable speed, no questions, no solicitations, no fuss. The waiting carriage and escort and the prompt journey to the cell implied that advance preparations had been made for its smooth execution. Obviously, I had been led into a trap, and it had been sprung on me.

Having groped my way to the narrow, hard bunk with which the cell was furnished, I lay down, massaging my head, which had not been split but had acquired a sizeable bump.

I cast my mind over the evening's sequence of events. Whichever view I took, nothing made undoubted sense. I had been on my guard from the moment my guide had taken the astonishing step of showing me the experimental laboratory, but the trap which I had anticipated had been a verbal one, a false proposition to test my response. I had been ready to affect innocent surprise and an inability to understand the implication of whatever offer was made to me. Such negative behaviour, I had been sure, would satisfy my guide's test. He would simply have led me back downstairs to rejoin the orchestra. His report to the superiors who had arranged for all this would be that I was merely what I professed to be, an artless English

137

idler indulging his eccentricity in a continental sojourn. The risk of showing me the interior of the forbidden room had been nil anyway: there had been nothing exceptional in it to see, no chance to tamper with anything, and no papers left lying about to steal.

Yet no sooner had I crossed the threshold than he had knocked me unconscious with the bottle with which, it now occurred to me, he had armed himself so innocently but purposefully. The obvious inference followed: he had set me up, as my old Pinkerton colleagues would have put it. He had lured me into forbidden territory and knocked me out. I would be found there conveniently as an intruder caught in the act.

Now, this was interesting. I sat up and thought hard about it. Had he been acting on his own initiative, seeking commendation for his sharp wits and prompt action, which would gain him some reward? Or had he been under orders? If the latter, whose orders, and in consequence of what suspicion, or accusation – or even betrayal?

This last thought brought me up with a jolt: Moriarty!

Once I remarked to Watson, apropos some crime bearing Moriarty's undoubted style, 'You can tell an old master by the sweep of his brush'; and if ever I thought I recognized that same brushwork, it was now. For some time he had been behaving in a manner which had attracted my notice: shiftily, nervously, unlike his usually phlegmatic, brooding self. His equipping himself with that sophisticated walking-stick rifle had strengthened my certainty that some action was being plotted within that great dome of a cranium.

Mycroft, feeling secure in his hold over him, had identified a prize for him, and put him into a position from which to launch himself at it. There were just two main obstacles: the Germans and me. After long and patient consideration, Moriarty had come to the conclusion that one of them was insuperable but that the other was expendable – and that other was myself.

In all this time – we were well into our second year of our mission – no gratuitous luck had come our way. We dared not make any move without it, yet none seemed remotely likely to crop up. Trying to put myself in his place, I imagined that at some point, a few weeks ago, Moriarty had had enough of inactivity. He had decided at last to throw in his lot with the Germans.

He would have had to proceed with caution, nonetheless. An approach to them behind my back, telling them frankly who he was, explaining how he had apparently risen from the dead, convincing them of his professional credentials, and offering his services to further the research begun by Hertz and Braun, would be no mere formality of a clandestine appointment, an interview, and a welcoming handshake. The rigid-minded Germans would have been instantly suspicious of a trick.

Yet, I could picture him persevering. His capacity for betrayal had shown itself clearly enough in the way he had left his entire organization to its fate, while accepting the means of saving himself.

He could stand to gain much. If the Germans did accept him, he would be free of Mycroft's hold over him. He would exchange sham nonentity for his old status of eminent scholar, perhaps becoming accepted and acclaimed in this homeland of science to a degree which he had been denied in his own. Not least, by compromising me, he could take the personal revenge which I had no doubt he still desired.

At one point during my night in the cell I heard a scuffling in the passage, and what I believed was Moriarty's complaining voice, soon stifled by a door's slam. It seemed all of a piece. They would naturally go through the motions of arresting him, for appearances' sake.

He and I had scowled at one another when we were brought face to face in the Police Chief's office. I felt grimy and out of place in my evening clothes. Inferior coffee and black bread had provided a sour breakfast.

'I am waiting, Herr Fisher,' the Chief now prompted me. His manner made it plain that he proposed to believe nothing I was going to tell him, and that he had other preoccupations. He had opened the interrogation by flatly stating that I had been found forcing my way into a forbidden part of the Schloss on the previous evening. Inquiries had revealed how I had contrived entry to the Schloss itself. Luckily, the observant usher, curious about the presence of an Englishman among the orchestra, had made it his business to watch me during the interludes and had seen me sneak off into the inner regions.

He had followed me, and caught me in the act of entering a room clearly marked out of bounds. The inference was obvious – I was a spy.

'It is all offensive nonsense,' I commenced my statement. 'I was invited to deputize by one of the violinists who had often heard me play. Any number of them had heard me, and will testify that I am a bona fide performer on the instrument.'

'I dare say they will, and I expect you are,' drawled the Chief. 'You could scarcely have used that trick if you were not, so I shall not put you to the trouble of demonstrating your ability. Proceed.'

'The gentleman here welcomed me most courteously,' I indicated the usher. 'I told him I was interested to be visiting a Schloss for the first time, and he offered to show me round in one of the interludes.'

'And led you to a room which is forbidden to all except those with business in it?'

He glanced towards the usher, who spread his hands and made a wry grimace, as if to affirm the absurdity of it all. The Chief nodded agreement with the usher and turned his sardonic look on me again.

'Whatever his motive,' I insisted, 'he unlocked the door with his own key and showed me into the room. Then he knocked me over the head from behind with the champagne bottle he was carrying.'

The usher spoke up. 'As soon as my suspicions were aroused and I decided to follow him I thought I had better not go empty handed, in case he should be armed. I seized the bottle as the only weapon available. Fortunately, as your Honour knows, champagne bottles are thick and heavy.'

'You are saying, then, that you did not accompany me?' I questioned him.

'Absurd. I followed you unseen.'

'Did I try any doors – seem to be searching for a particular room? Might I not have been seeking a toilet?'

'You knew where you were making for. You went straight there without pausing.'

'And how, precisely, did I gain entry?'

'A key. A skeleton key, no doubt?'

'Which was subsequently found on me?' I asked the Chief, turning on him sharply, so that he stiffened in his chair.

'No doubt it is among the items collected as exhibits,' he answered. 'I myself have not yet examined them...'

'Then it's a pity, sir, because you would have found no skeleton key.'

'Well, we shall see, by and by.'

Yes, I thought, you had overlooked that detail; but you will have plenty of time to repair the omission.

'So,' I readdressed the usher, 'you were thoroughly convinced by now that your suspicions were justified?'

He sneered. His manner this morning was quite different from the previous evening. 'Who would not have been convinced?'

'Just so. And, in the courage of your conviction, you sprang forward and struck me unconscious with your champagne bottle.'

'I judged I had to act without delay. As I have said, you might have been armed.'

To the surprise of the note-taking policeman, I addressed myself to him.

'Will you please be so kind as to confirm from your notes that it was I who first mentioned the champagne bottle a short while ago?'

The man glanced at the Chief for approval. Receiving no sign he leafed back a page, found the place, and read out my words: ' "He unlocked the door with his own key and showed me into the room. Then he knocked me over the head from behind with the champagne bottle he was carrying." '

'That is the first reference to the precise object with which I was struck?'

'Yes, sir.'

'I am obliged to you.' I turned back to the usher. 'I wonder whether you have some explanation of how I was able to describe this morning the weapon which you used last night but, according to your account, had no chance to see?'

'I, er ... That's just a quibble.'

'Oh, no. It is a pertinent observation. You say you took me by surprise from behind, knocking me unconscious. How did I know that you used a champagne bottle, if you had not already let me see you with it?'

'Bravo!' said a surprising voice at my side. 'Very good, Mr Fisher.'

I had to stare at Moriarty, who was managing to nod and oscillate simultaneously, in the grip of undisguised admiration. It was his turn to address the Chief of Police.

'You see, sir, this whole affair is either a monstrous misunderstanding, or there has been some plot to discredit my friend. It is bad enough for myself, being dragged from my bed in the dark of night and subjected to the indignity of a prison cell; but my friend has suffered physical injury in addition.'

I had so convinced myself of his part in this obvious plot to discredit me and so free him from my watch over him that I was even more surprised by what the Police Chief said next, springing from his chair to stride his room as if it were indeed a stage setting, and with an animation which I should not have imagined from this grey man.

'Silence, the pair of you! Do you think I am prepared to sit here and listen to these proceedings being dictated by a pair of culprits?'

'You are mistaken, sir,' I put in mildly. 'As I have been at pains to explain . . .'

'*Silence!* You are spies. English spies. You know it and I know it. We have suspected as much almost from the time of your arrival in Karlsruhe. The elderly headmaster and his trusty assistant wishing to study mathematics! If it were not pathetic, I should laugh.'

He evidently concluded that it was not so pathetic after all, and indulged himself in a burst of histrionic laughter, as startling as the rattle of a quick-firing gun.

'So naive,' he chuckled. 'So trusting. We were content to leave you untroubled, to let you waste your time, for there was nothing you could do. It was not until we were informed that you proposed making an attempt on the Schloss. . . . Ah, I see a genuine response from you at last. But if you will keep company with disgusting Russians nothing should surprise you. You disappoint me, gentlemen. I have great respect for the English, and previous agents of yours with whom I have had to deal in a long career have struck me as both highly efficient and charming. But to think of confiding your plans to a malodorous creature such as that Azeff, even to the point of seeking his assistance . . . .'

He flung up his arms and let them flop to his sides, in a gesture of hopelessness, before throwing himself into his chair.

'We protest most strongly against any such insinuations,' said Moriarty. 'Don't we, Mr Fisher?'

'Most certainly, Mr Etherage. For the benefit of the record of this interview, sir, we wish it known that it was Azeff who broached to us the idea of himself entering the Schloss. He thought of writing to the Ochrana and proposing a deal.'

The Chief laughed again. 'What a cloud of birds with one stone! I am inclined to believe you. But such a man! When he came here to inform against you – for a fee, of course – we found him so repellent, and his story so unlikely, that we held him while we investigated it.'

'In that case you must have found that he was lying.'

'Perhaps so; but he proved to have his uses, all the same. We had not so far troubled to search your belongings, but now we decided to do so. Yours in particular Mr Etherage proved most revealing. I need only instance your copy of *Wiedemann's Annalen* 34, 1888, with the Herr Dr Hertz's paper on electromagnetic waves so heavily annotated in what we have confirmed is your own hand. *Plus* many pages of notes and formulae of your own, which we have had assessed by our scientists. I have the report here. They pronounce your calculations interesting and displaying mathematical skills of an exceptionally high order. You have evidently benefited from your studies at our distinguished Polytechnic, Mr Etherage.'

'*Thank* you,' said Moriarty heavily.

'Not at all. For your information, though, our scientists confirm that your efforts, while praiseworthy, represent no advance on their own work. That is as well for you, for otherwise I should be placed in some embarrassment in the matter of dealing with you both. As it is, I am happy to tell you that I can be lenient. In fact, we'll have some coffee in. Rauber!' He motioned to one of the soldiers, who went out.

The Chief was relaxed and enjoying himself now.

'We were not too happy about that walking-stick gun of yours which appeared recently. Azeff's information coming on top of that really forced us to take action. I regret the intrusion into your private effects, but it was necessary.'

'I hope,' I said, 'you didn't pay that villain for his dirty trick. That was what it was, you know.'

'Oh, I'm sure. No, all he got was his railway fare to take him out of Germany. As soon as we had satisfied ourselves about you two we escorted him to the frontier, about a week ago.' He sighed. 'I fear he will prove a thorn in someone's side some day, that one, but we had nothing on him.'

The coffee arrived, smelling delicious this time, and we accepted it thankfully. Our game was up, and we all knew it. There was nothing for it but acceptance that Moriarty and I were the subjects of what my friends in the London criminal fraternity would term 'a fair cop'. Even the castle usher, whom I was sure was a police detective, apologized to me for having had to strike his blow.

'I could not risk a struggle, and perhaps getting bested,' he explained.

'At least we enjoyed the champagne first,' I laughed, but he was not to be trapped. He merely smiled, and turned away.

The Chief said expansively, 'I do not propose to embarrass you further, gentlemen. I am quite satisfied that you are what you are, but that you have achieved nothing deleterious to my country and used no violence against any of its nationals. Of course, if you insist on being put on public trial . . . . No, I imagined not. In that case, you will be escorted to your lodgings and then to the frontier. I trust Switzerland would be most convenient, being closest?'

We agreed.

'Good. And you may keep your gun, Mr Etherage. A beautiful piece. Von Herder, I presume? Yes, I thought as much. Be thankful that you did not make any use of it while on German soil, though. Things might have turned out very differently for you both. And now, another cup of coffee?'

Mission Ended

————

THE GERMAN train carried us along precisely the opposite route to that which we had originally followed. Two detectives in plain clothes travelled with us in our reserved first-class compartment. They were affable and studiedly courteous. At their diffident request, Moriarty demonstrated the unfolding of his walking-stick gun, so that they and I were able to admire its ingenious construction and method of working. They had insisted that it remained unloaded while we were on German territory, but had not confiscated the miniature bullets.

At Basle, they shook hands warmly with us and made an almost jocular farewell. Then they departed for the train to take them back to Karlsruhe. We ate luncheon in the excellent station buffet, and in due course boarded a Swiss train which would carry us to Zurich.

Taking care not to ruffle Moriarty's feathers, I had assumed tacit control of our movements in the light of the changed situation. From Basle I telegraphed to Steiler at the Englischer Hof in Meiringen, to say that we should be coming there. Zurich was out of our way, but I preferred to take the extra trouble in case the Germans had put an agent on to us, curious to find out where we should make for and with whom we might get in touch. I explained to Moriarty that we could more easily shake off any 'shadow' in the bigger city of Zurich than in Lucerne, and would be wise to stay there for a day or two before going on to Meiringen by another route. He accepted my decision without demur. I also cabled in cipher to Mycroft, telling him of our decision to lie up in the obscurity of Meiringen pending his further orders.

We had a first-class compartment to ourselves on the train to Zurich, and I noticed that Moriarty lost no time in reloading his gun. He had seemed ill at ease in Basle, and glad to leave. He remarked that he would be glad to be in Meiringen again.

Basle, Switzerland's second most populous city, lying where her frontiers converge with those of Germany and France. It was here that 'Etherage' and I were released from German custody following our arrest and expulsion.

It was on the tip of my tongue to ask if he had any reason for saying that, and why he should consider it necessary to rearm himself at the first opportunity. I was going to add that he had nothing to fear from me, and challenge him with any intent he might be harbouring of using his gun on me. Despite the Karlsruhe Chief of Police's assurances, I was still not wholly convinced that my companion was innocent of some plot, perhaps even in association with Azeff. I suppose something of the spy mentality had rubbed off on me, and had left me conditioned never again to accept anyone or any circumstance at face value. Perhaps it is an asset in detective work, but an excess of cynicism and scepticism cannot be very improving to the character and, contrary to a widespread impression which I blame Watson for propagating, I do not believe that by nature I was always so cold and unimpressionable as I have seen myself depicted.

146

I was about to ask my travelling companion if his sometimes nervous behaviour had any definable cause, and try to reassure him, but he forestalled me by broaching another topic.

'Now that we are alone at last, Mr Holmes, permit me to say that I attach no blame to you for what happened. I believe entirely that we were betrayed by the wretch Azeff for what he could get out of it, but that he had no idea how near to the truth he was in picking upon us. If we made a mistake, it was in letting our contempt for him show. That, and his obvious hatred of our nationality, caused him to use us.'

I thought this an opportune chance to remind him that I was not so gullible as perhaps he had come to suppose.

'I am pleased to hear you say that, Professor. I confess I had entertained some suspicion that you were implicated in the matter yourself.'

'Dear me, Mr Holmes, dear me! Such a notion! Believe me, had I undertaken to compromise you, I should have made a far more thorough job of it. You would not be travelling free now if I had delivered you up to the Germans. You would have been settling down to a long gaol sentence, if not facing a firing squad. I absolve you of incompetence in stepping into that trap; I trust you will not repay me by seeking to lay the blame for our failure at my door. It would be unworthy of you, not to mention wholly false.'

'Then I apologize, Professor,' I felt moved to say. 'In any case, recriminations will not serve us. We should do better to review what small results we have got to lay before my brother, even if they are negative ones.'

'I agree. To begin with, you noticed how that chief of police took pains to assure me that my calculations were futile? Might that not have been his bluff, to dissuade me from trying to proceed further?'

'It's possible. Speaking of that, Professor, don't you think it was just a trifle remiss of you to leave your documents where they could find them?'

Moriarty's eyes flashed angrily for once as he snapped back: 'Do you suppose they were lying on my dressing-table? I was quite aware that they had been examined, but I supposed that you had been making another of your raids, only with rather more thoroughness. Oh, don't deny it. I have always known that you were prying into my things.'

'Well,' I smiled, trying to restore his better humour, 'you have certainly not been slow to return the compliment.' A thought had arisen to puzzle me. 'Let us be frank, though. I had never noticed any copy of Hertz's paper among your things, let alone calculations of your own. I think I should have risked counselling caution if I had.'

'You missed the papers because your searches were kept within the bounds of discretion, as I hope you will concede were mine. You did not cut into my trunk linings.'

'Which they did?'

'I kept the papers there, restitching them carefully in after each use, which was not often. In recent times I have noticed you regarding me with a new expression – degree of perplexity, shall we say? When I found that the lining had been cut and the papers obviously removed and replaced, I believed that whatever you had become so curious about had got the better of you, and you had abandoned caution and made your latest search a more rigorous one.'

With the stem of my pipe I tapped his cane, which rested against his seat, beside his legs. 'That was the cause of my curiosity, Professor. That and . . .'

I hesitated, but he raised an inquiring eyebrow. I thought that the time had come to be blunt. '. . . your increasing anxiety. I first saw signs of it when you showed yourself so eager about the English newspapers. Understandably, you were anxious to follow the reports of the trials of your people, and presumably concerned lest your own name should be brought up, after all. I, too, read the reports, and noted that, as I had expected, you were not once mentioned. The number of trials began to dwindle, yet not your anxiety over them. By the set of your lips when you had finished reading each case, and the way you would cast the newspaper aside and fall to brooding, I observed that your concern, far from receding, was growing. What was it that you had sought in vain, and were now, to your distress, giving up hope of finding? Scarcely the mention of some crime which had not come to light, but more likely of a member of your gang who, from the absence of his name from the reports, you knew must have escaped the net?'

'Mr Holmes,' said Moriarty, 'I have entertained harsh opinions of you, but I have never doubted your perspicacity. Allow me to compliment you on your deductive process.'

'Superficial,' I murmured.

'By your standards, perhaps; but nevertheless correct, although I am a little disappointed that you do not carry your deduction to its end.'

'Ah,' I said. 'The gun.'

'Precisely. When you visited von Herder's workshop after me that day . . .'

'You saw me!'

'Naturally. I never turn a corner of a street without looking back to see who might be following. I glimpsed you, and waited to watch you go in.'

'I assure you, Professor, I had not followed you there. It was pure chance – and curiosity.'

'I must admit to having felt quite piqued at the time. However, you made amends by your civility in pretending to recognize nothing out of the ordinary about my new cane.'

'It did occur to me to wonder whether it was for eventual use against myself, nonetheless.'

'It is natural that you would. I chose to leave you guessing about that.'

'Perhaps I am still guessing, Professor.'

'Understandably. Circumstances generally dictate these things.'

'On the other hand, I discarded the notion some time ago. It occurred to me that, should you wish to kill or harm me, you had ample opportunity without needing so elaborate a weapon. To complete my deduction, then, your disappointment at the lack of something in the newpaper reports, your growing signs of anxiety when travelling about, and your acquisition of a weapon which could accompany you everywhere, and always be in your hand when out of doors, ready for instantaneous use – all of it added up to . . .'

'Yes?'

'There is some member of your organization still at large whom you would prefer not to meet. He is no insignificant pawn of yours, but a senior figure, for you know that he would recognize you, which lesser fry would not. He travels about a good deal, or else you would not expect to run across him outside England. And if he should find you, either by chance or, suspecting that you are still alive, by tracking you down, you will need to defend your life. In short, you deserted him to face

the music with the rest, but you did not take the precaution of
ensuring that he would be incriminated with them and so put
away where he cannot harm you. There, Professor, is that
enough for you?'

He sank back against his seat cushions with a groan.

'More than enough. You are correct in every detail.'

Our train rattled along a valley, the track sharing direction
with a slender river. It was a bright afternoon of blue sky,
green meadow grass, neat Swiss dwellings, and a distant vista
of peaks. I saw from my watch that we should arrive in Zurich
while it was still daylight. I could understand now with what
apprehension Moriarty must view each new destination,
among whose throngs might chance to be a man with hatred
in his heart who would not hesitate to kill him on sight.

'There have been moments when I have almost been tempted
to confide in you, Mr Holmes,' confessed Moriarty. 'Old habits
die hard, though, and I dare say the truth of it is that I have
trusted you no more than you have trusted me. Now that I am
aware how close you have come to the facts by your own
deductions, I will, if you will listen, fill in the details which you
lack. After all,' he added sardonically, 'you are by way of
being my bodyguard, in view of your brother's vested interest
in my life. Failing a bullet from the blue, against which there
is no defence, there will at least be a double chance of avoiding
a confrontation if you, too, know with whom we are dealing.'

I nodded. 'It takes a brave man to admit that he is afraid,
Professor. I think it was perhaps your pride, rather than
mistrust, which prevented your telling me this before.'

'As you wish. Do you know of Colonel Sebastian Moran?'

'The name means nothing.'

'There – you see? I have kept him as much out of the lime-
light as myself, and for the same reasons. Your energies have
been concentrated on hounding me, to the extent that you
have quite missed noticing him. Well, I suppose you would call
him my lieutenant. Like myself, he attained eminence in his
own sphere, but was hounded out of it by jealous humbugs.
In his case, it was nonentities who could never hope to match
him for physical bravery. They conspired to accuse him of
cheating at cards in his regiment's mess. Despite his denials,
he was required by his general to sign an undertaking never to
gamble again. Moran refused, and resigned from the army.'

150

'A somewhat headstrong gesture, surely?'

'In keeping with his nature. A man who could crawl down a drain after a wounded man-eating tiger to finish the beast off would scarcely stand for pettifogging disciplining over a mere game of cards.'

'At which he *had* been cheating, no doubt?'

Moriarty stared back, and then laughed out. 'I am quite sure. In keeping with his nature again.'

'I should not have thought, Professor, that a man of such headstrong temperament would provide you with an ideal partner in your line of work.'

'Be that as it may, he proved his value to me in many ways. He is not a type of man of whom I could ever make a personal friend. He is arrogant, fierce, violent-tempered; the more so, I expect, for having had his career ruined. He will be only just into his fifties now, and could have attained the highest rank. You will find all his details when you next have access to *Who's Who*. As well as a soldier, his reputation as a big-game hunter is second to none.'

'And now you fear he may be hunting you.'

'I do not know. If the legend of my death has held, he will presumably have believed it like everyone else. It is if he should find that I am still alive that he will become a danger.'

'He evidently wasn't arrested,' I pointed out. 'He has nothing to blame you with.'

'I failed to warn him of the impending police action. Before I could do so, your brother had summoned me to our meeting at the Diogenes Club, and afterwards it was no longer in my power to confide in Moran. I should have had to tell him that I was to "disappear", and why, and I could not have trusted such a man with secrets of that kind.'

'When he subsequently read of your supposed death, he would surely have assumed that you had left hastily in pursuit of me, but perished in the course of it.'

'Knowing Moran, it is much more likely that he will think I betrayed him first – that I fled the country, and that it was you who pursued me. He will have assumed that I thought only of my own skin, and left him to take his chance with the rest.'

'Well, he seems to have got away with it. Let us hope that thankfulness for that will have mellowed him, and he will have forgotten any grudge.'

151

'As you say, you do not know Colonel Sebastian Moran.'

'Then we shall simply have to be vigilant. But is there any reason why he should be here, of all places? Switzerland does not exactly abound in man-eating tigers.'

'You are right, of course. But the world is a small one, and concern for one's life has a way of seeming to diminish it.'

'You did well to confide in me, Professor. Pray do not hold back, should you have the least cause to suspect a sighting.'

'Thank you, Mr Holmes. But to get back to *our* reason for being here, have you thought hard whether there might not be something, however small, to show for our failed mission?'

I had to admit that for most of the wretched night in the cell my mind had been busy with recriminations, based largely on hypothetical assumptions, in which he himself figured. Since then, I had been too occupied for constructive thought.

'In any case,' I admitted, 'what could there be? I know where the laboratory is situated inside the Schloss, but I had virtually deduced that in advance. I have only a vague recollection of its appearance and its contents.'

'Tell me,' he urged. 'Focus your memory's eye and think hard. Any detail whatsoever.'

Haltingly, I dragged back what detail I could from those few seconds' perception within the room. Since our mission began I had naturally read up what little I could find about the production of electricity, and seen diagrams of some of the quite rudimentary apparatus used for experiments. It had enabled me to recognize the zinc plates with their polished brass rods and spheres, together with the copper-coated Leyden jars and their wiring, as constituting an oscillatory circuit.

Moriarty shook his head. 'Formulae are the apparatus I understand,' he said gloomily. 'The great composers did not require to work at the keyboard to create even the most striking and complex of their effects: they did it in their minds, and with pencil and pad. That is the way I work, too. If a thing is capable of being formularized, it can be made to work.'

'The dainty green of the spring below, the virgin white of the winter above.' The Wetterhorn overlooks the village of Meiringen, where the Englischer Hof was Watson's and my last brief abode together, although I spent much time there later with 'Etherage'.

'There was what I took to be an antenna,' I added, groping on. 'Just an arm attached horizontally to an upright rod, with various wires attached.'

'Well, we had taken it for granted that they were looking for means of sending waves directionally. That is where the antenna would come in, so it tells us nothing in itself. The room was at the top of the Schloss, no doubt at the rear, where there would be an uninterrupted field over open country.'

I hesitated, closing my eyes for some moments as I strove to recapture what I had seen. Suddenly my searching gaze seemed to lift away from the dimly-remembered details, to take in the room itself. It traversed it, as my first glance must have done, upon the opening of the door and the switching on of the light. I opened my eyes again and stared at Moriarty, who was watching me, hunched in his seat, his head resting against the cushion and for once almost still.

'No,' I said. 'No. There was no uninterrupted field. The room had no windows.'

He shot forward almost with a spring, the nervous movement of his neck reasserting itself immediately.

'You are sure?' he demanded. 'No windows at all? They were not merely closed or concealed?'

It was my turn to shake my head, and firmly.

'Where a window had been there were metal sheets. I can visualize them quite plainly on every wall, in fact. Sheets of metal, covering the greater surface of every wall.'

Slowly, on Moriarty's countenance, there appeared once more that cunning, closed-mouth smile which, together with his oscillations, had led me in the past to term him reptilian.

'Mr Holmes,' he said, and his eyes gleamed with rekindled enthusiasm; 'You saw precisely what we needed to see. Our mission has been successful.'

'THE SECOND MOST DANGEROUS MAN'

THE INQUIRER who searches the scientific libraries for records of Professor James Moriarty's work in furtherance of that of Dr Heinrich Hertz, concerning the propagation of electro-magnetic waves in air and their reflection, will be wasting his time. Among all that has been published on the subject, his name never once appears.

It would be the cause of continuing chagrin to him, were he still living; but it had all along been part of Mycroft's bargain with him, struck that night at the Diogenes Club, that if he would undertake the patriotic mission offered him as an alternative to arrest and as a means of atoning for his past misdemeanours, he would be exempted from retribution. His death had long been presumed, in association with my own. My return to the world of the living was all along intended, and it was necessary that I have a good enough explanation for what had happened. But, as Oscar Wilde might have expressed it through Lady Bracknell, to retrieve one dead man might be regarded as fortunate; to produce both still alive would look decidedly fishy.

Moriarty had agreed reluctantly that his only future could be under a new identity. As his awareness grew of the poten-tial hazard of chancing to meet Colonel Moran, I imagine he came more to welcome the arrangement. His physical charac-teristics virtually dictated his staying abroad, 'condemned to wander like the Flying Dutchman, forever', he remarked to me in a moment of introspective gloom, but at least it would give him a better chance of living out his days unharmed. 'I have saved my life, but lost my identity,' he sighed. 'Well, so be it. Let Etherage prevail.'

The name Etherage, however, does not appear in the scientific annals either – or at least, if it does, it relates to some other man entirely, and has no connection with this affair. In order to explain why, I had better continue this narrative in full.

We reached Meiringen safely to find that the village had been devastated by fire not long after Watson and I had stayed there, but that the Englischer Hof had survived. Moriarty wanted nothing more than the solitude of his room in order to get on with his calculations, whose nature he preferred not to discuss. He had the mathematical bit firmly between his teeth now, and I was happy to leave him to it. Although Steiler had had many visitors to the Englischer Hof in the two and more years since our 'deaths' – the hotel where I and Watson had spent our last night together had become something of a place of pilgrimage, together with the ledge above the Reichenbach Falls – none had come asking the sort of questions which betrayed suspicions about the truth of what had happened between Moriarty and me. Without going into details, I warned him to be on the lookout for anyone whom he sensed might have followed us here this time.

The one person who did come to see us, less than a week after our arrival, was my brother Mycroft. As at any time, it was a considerable surprise to meet him beyond his closely defined London environs. It made him seem quite a different person, with his town clothes exchanged for country wear; but he still carried his aura of sedentary habits and over-indulgence.

I gave him a detailed report of all that had occurred. He offered neither criticism nor praise, rebuke nor sympathy; he merely kept nodding his head, making a concertina effect with his chins.

'And Moriarty is convinced that he has enough to go upon now to achieve positive results?' he said, when I had done. Our conversation was tête-à-tête, in Steiler's private apartments in the hotel.

'He's working like a demon at whatever it is,' I answered. 'It is all I can do to coax him down to meals.'

'I trust his results and workings are securely hidden away when he is out of his room,' Mycroft rejoined sharply. 'What about night-time? Have you made sure that no one could get in while he is asleep?'

'One doesn't sleep with the windows open in this air,' I laughed. 'His room is next to mine, on the upper floor, and Steiler has arranged an emergency bell between us. All visitors to the hotel are scrutinized with the greatest care. There is no reason to suppose that anything untoward will be tried.'

'It might be safer to take him back to England, all the same,' Mycroft pondered. 'Our people could guard him.'

'He feels perfectly secure here, Mycroft – more so than he would at home. It would be different for me. I could live for months in disguise if need be, and go anywhere I chose. No one who had ever known the Professor would fail to recognize him in a flash.'

'He will have to stay on abroad when all this is over, you know. We cannot arrange another resurrection.'

'He understands that. Besides, I believe he genuinely wishes to turn his back on his old connections, and former surroundings might carry too many associations for his peace of mind. There is just one thing which worries me.'

I proceeded to tell him about Colonel Sebastian Moran.

'While the Professor is working at full stretch I doubt that he even gives him a thought. If he's idle, though, he has leisure to imagine that Moran and he will come face to face at any moment. He goes so far as to term the Colonel the second most dangerous man in London. Modesty, of course, prevents his naming the first.'

'You must make yourself responsible that they don't,' Mycroft said gravely. 'We can't have anything happening to our tame genius at this stage.'

'You know nothing of this Moran yourself?'

'As a matter of fact, I do, though not in connection with Moriarty. He plays cards occasionally at the Baldwin Club. It's just a minute or so from the Diogenes, so I can look in without inconvenience when I feel inclined.'

'What does he look like?'

'In his early fifties. Rather debauched-looking. A gaunt, heavily-lined face, with a massive brow and an equally massive moustache. It makes for a pretty fierce-looking specimen, though distinctly stooped. I dare say he cut a finer figure in his army days than now.'

Mycroft spent an hour alone with Moriarty, and later the three of us dined together, still keeping well away from the public gaze. Moriarty was able to supply further information about his erstwhile 'chief of staff', as he affected to term Colonel Moran.

'He is a well-educated man, for a professional soldier – Eton and Oxford. His late father was once Minister to Persia, Sir Augustus Moran, CB.'

'Of course, of course!' Mycroft recalled. 'Where does he live? Has he any other clubs, beside the Baldwin?'

'He has a bachelor apartment in Kensington, behind the Albert Hall. His other clubs, let me see – the Anglo-Indian, the Tankerville, and some other card place – the Bagatelle.'

'I have heard of it; the sort of place where the stakes are far higher than allowed at the Baldwin where I lose my modest half-crown at whist.'

'Once a cheat, always a cheat?' I suggested.

'I see what you mean, Sherlock. I will have inquiries made. It would be useful to gain some hold over this fellow, so that we might legitimately detain him for questioning should we ever find it convenient. Professor, I ask you again, in the interest of your own safeguarding, is there no more serious crime you could ascribe to him which would enable me to have him removed from circulation?'

Moriarty pondered for a time before answering heavily.

'I am afraid not, Mr Holmes. The only major witness for a successful prosecution would be myself – and the difficulties as to that are obvious.'

'Ah, well. . . . Tell me, does he go armed, should you say?'

Again Moriarty hesitated.

'Whether he carries a pistol, I cannot say,' he replied after quite a long pause.

'There is something else, Professor,' I said. 'You are holding something back.'

'Well . . . the air-gun.'

'An air-gun?'

'It is . . . not quite an air-gun. A rifle which works on that principle, only much more powerful. It shoots revolver bullets, but it is almost silent.'

'I never heard of such a thing,' admitted Mycroft, and drank some of the excellent Swiss wine. Moriarty said nothing.

'If I am not mistaken,' I said, 'I see the hand of von Herder again. A blind mechanic in Munich,' I explained to Mycroft.

'A genius at his craft. I am sure that the Professor would be willing to demonstrate an example of it.'

I looked significantly at the silver-topped cane, propped against Moriarty's chair. He looked almost sheepish.

'You are right, of course, Mr Holmes. Von Herder made the air-rifle some four years ago.'

'Also in the form of a stick?'

'No. It folds up.'

'I think,' said Mycroft, 'I should get our people to look at the weapon you describe. There might be enough to warrant its confiscation. Law-abiding citizens do not go about armed in that fashion.'

'I beg you not to,' Moriarty said. 'Only I could have told you of its existence, so if approached about it he would know at once where your information came from.'

'A good point, Professor. At least, though, we can ensure that if he travels anywhere our people at the ports can watch for it. If it were to be found on him as 'twere by accident, he would have no grounds for suspicion.'

Moriarty brightened. 'Ah, yes. That would be quite in order. A keen mind, Mr Holmes, a keen mind.'

Mycroft beamed, and the two actually raised their glasses to one another. Looking at my stout, pink-faced brother, and the lean, pallid man who faced him across the table, I thought about the qualities they had in common, and how equally equipped intellectually each was for the other's role. I knew how devious my brother's methods could be, even ruthless if circumstances dictated, and what a formidable criminal he could have made. The same has been said of myself, but I fancy that Mycroft, gone wrong, could have outstripped me in a career of evil. For all his jelly-like appearance, his indolent posture, his manner of speaking, so languid at times as to give the impression that even conversation was too great a physical effort for him, and that he would have infinitely preferred to communicate solely by telepathy – for all these pretensions to inactivity and sloth, his brain was razor-sharp and ever alert. When he was apparently doing least, he was more than likely doing most; but it did not show, and it was a considerable deception for the unwary.

Moriarty was starting to fidget, and soon asked leave to get back to his work. Mycroft did not trouble to request a demonstration of the stick-gun. He shook hands with Moriarty, wished him success, and let him go. He looked at his watch.

'I must be on the afternoon train, Sherlock,' he said. 'The Prime Minister is waiting anxiously for my report.'

'Did you manage to get out of Moriarty what precisely he is up to?'

'Oh, yes. He was reluctant for a time, but I reminded him that he is answerable to me personally, and that I had not come all this way merely to inquire after his health.'

'Well, then?'

'What, Sherlock?'

'You are going to tell me, surely?'

'Oh, I don't think that would be in order. Not right at all.'

'If you don't, I shall accompany you back to London, without disguise, and walk down Fleet Street in broad daylight.'

He sighed, but capitulated.

'The principle of transmitting waves was established by Hertz, working from the earlier theories of Clerk Maxwell and others. Our own people have made a good deal of progress down that same road. So, no doubt, have the French, the Italians, and any others who troubled to study Hertz's publication of his researches before the Germans made them secret. But Hertz had demonstrated not only that waves may be propagated, but that they are capable of being reflected back. By the lucky chance of your noticing that the laboratory walls were blank, and metal-covered, you gave Moriarty what he was seeking. What is preoccupying them at Karlsruhe is the sending of a wave, and receiving that same wave back – hence the metal walls, being used as reflectors.'

'I don't see much value in that.'

'No, Sherlock. As one who professes not to care how the Solar System works so long as it continues to do so, you could hardly be expected to imagine what a reflected electromagnetic wave might achieve. Suppose it is transmitted in a directional beam, which can be swept about until it comes up against metal and is reflected back to its source. . . .'

'Good heavens! You are inferring the detection of warships?'

'Precisely. It is the metal ships which we and all the major powers are building now which make this discovery the greatest leap forward since the invention of the monostatic range-finder, but far more advanced. A chain of transmitting

'The Prime Minister is waiting anxiously for my report.' Gladstone was in his last ministry when my brother Mycroft informed him of 'Etherage's' momentous findings late in 1893. It had been his predecessor, Lord Salisbury, who had sanctioned Mycroft's masterly deception two years earlier.

points around our coastline, and we need never fear invasion again. Moriarty assures me that the system will work equally well in darkness or even the thickest fog. An approaching armada would be detected long before it could reach our coasts. He says it should be possible for ships themselves to carry the equipment, and hunt down one another with it.'

'I am deeply impressed. I had no idea. But surely, it becomes urgently necessary to find out how far the Germans have actually got with this?'

161

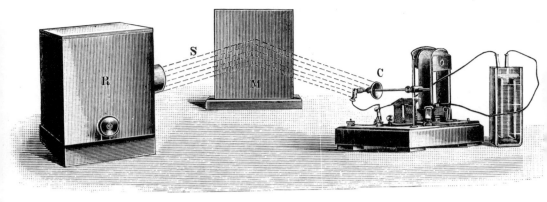

Demonstrating Clerk Maxwell's contention that a metallic surface should reflect electromagnetic waves. Waves from the resonator on the right rebound from the metal mirror and are received by the opposite resonator. The implications caused the German government to make the work secret.

'It would be desirable, but I see no means of achieving it, except by another lucky chance. We don't wish to tell our agents what to look for specifically, lest one of them turns his coat, or gets caught and interrogated to a degree that you were spared, and gives away that we are up to their secret. In Moriarty's opinion, we have little to worry about. He says they would scarcely be playing about in a room in Karlsruhe if they had progressed as far as sophisticated trials.'

'And he himself? What is he doing now?'

'He has identified several problems. The smallness of that laboratory, and the sort of figures put forward in Hertz's paper, suggest that the transmitted waves are too weak for practical purposes. They need some means of considerable intensification before they can range over long distances and cause sufficiently strong reflections to travel back to the receiving apparatus. He is seeking a means also of calculating the relationship between the time interval of the transmission and the receipt of its echo, and the distance of the reflecting object. He is doing it all mathematically, of course. When he is satisfied with his results, our scientists will take them into the laboratories and begin practical experiments.'

'And meanwhile we stay here in Meiringen?'

'Wherever you judge is safest for your charge, and where he can work without fear or interruption – especially violent interruption. I rely on you, Sherlock. And now I must be going.'

'You'll make inquiries about this Moran? He seems the only fly in the ointment.'

'He will be investigated at once, and detained if there is the least excuse.'

'How is the rest of the underworld faring in my absence?' I asked as we moved to the door.

'Oh, Scotland Yard continue to do their manly best. Their new building seems to have had a calming effect on the Metropolitan Police in general. They grumble less and there is less talk of militant action against the authorities.'

'The improved pay and pensions will have helped. How is the new Commissioner, Bradford, shaping?'

'Very well, unlike the run of some old India hands. He has actually visited every station in his manor and encouraged the men to air their opinions.'

'Good heavens!'

'New stations are being built, and old ones renovated. Lighter weight uniforms are allowed in summer, and sports clubs are being organized. To cap it all, though, they have their own independent weekly newspaper. *Police Review and Parade Gossip*, it is called.' Mycroft chuckled. 'There was something disparaging about you in the very first issue.'

'Disrespect for the dead!'

'Oh, and speaking of that, I saw your friend Inspector Lestrade the other day, though not to speak to. I hear he quite fancies that your mantle lies about his shoulders. "Mr Sherlock 'olmes, God rest 'is soul, would've done it this or that way, but that isn't my way o' goin' about it" sort of thing.'

We laughed, but I asked more gently, 'What of poor old Watson? Do you see him?'

'Never. He lost his wife, you know. Heart, I believe.'

'That sweet girl! I heard nothing.'

'Naturally, I couldn't have you informed. You might have been tempted to the indiscretion of a message of condolence, which he could have guessed came from you.'

'Poor Mary. Poor old Watson. I want no more of this work when this is over, Mycroft.'

'If all goes well, my boy, the spy's trade will be ended. The British Isles will be impregnable. Besides, who knows where

Col. Sir Edward Bradford, Commissioner of the Metropolitan Police 1890–1903. After a distinguished army career he had been head of the political and secret departments of the India Office. He dealt firmly with police militancy and discontentment, and many beneficial reforms ensued.

the electromagnetic spy may manage to take us in time – into the enemy's very back parlour, perhaps.'

'No more spies? You will die of boredom, Mycroft. Still, there remains the Diogenes Club. You can be sure of unceasing stimulus there.'

So we made our brotherly farewell, and I was left to resume my role of well-fed watchdog, while Watson pined, and Lestrade strutted, and teeming, criminal London called out for my attention.

'EUREKA!'

A DAY at last dawned – and dawned is the literal term, for it was barely daylight – when there came a hammering at my bedroom door in the Englischer Hof. I leaped out of bed to respond, immediately alert to any emergency.

When I had turned the key and opened the door it seemed at first that my fear was realized: Moriarty stood there in his dressing robe, his cheeks the colour of chalk, his tufts of hair straggling wildly from the sides of his head, the deep-set eyes almost immersed in the black pools which surrounded them.

But from those depths there shone a fire; and as he stepped swiftly across my threshold he flourished a small sheaf of papers, uttering the one word: 'Eureka!'

I bustled him back to his own room, afraid that in his excitement to come to me he might have left it unlocked and vulnerable. Even though the rest of the hotel lay still and silent, the passageway deserted in night's last shadow, no chances were worth risking. Surely enough, his door was wide open. Papers were scattered all over the counterpane on a bed in which he had clearly not slept.

He nodded a silent acknowledgment of his error, but gripped me by the shoulder with his free hand, as if thinking it might be necessary to shake me into realization that he had at last reached the solution to his calculations.

'Irrefutable!' he declared, without giving me the chance to ask if he was sure. 'It will be possible to locate a substantial metal object, such as a warship, and from the strength and direction of the reflected wave, to calculate its position exactly. Optical range-finding, save for small weapons firing over short distances, becomes obsolete at a stroke!'

'Congratulations, Professor!' I cried, and shook his hand, which was feverishly hot in contrast with his facial pallor. 'You have arrived at your conclusions suddenly?'

He nodded excitedly. 'It is so often the way with the sub-conscious mind, Mr Holmes. You yourself must have noticed that a problem grappled with over a lengthy period, and seemingly resistant to all that conscious effort can achieve, will often solve itself as suddenly as though there had been no difficulty at all – like a blockage being sluiced away before a wholly unlooked-for surge of inspiration.'

'A pound of black shag tobacco achieves much the same result in my case,' I smiled. 'But I know what you mean. The nature of inspiration remains one of the greatest studies awaiting man's solution, yet he will have to look to inspiration itself to give him the ultimate truth of it; and what shall we conclude from that?'

He paid no heed to my philosophizing.

'I was about to retire to bed, but paused to glance over my latest workings for the umpteenth time. Something made me linger over them, and the next thing I knew I had my answers. What is the time now?' He peered about, as though only just aware of the earliness of the hour.

'Half-past four,' I told him.

'Dear me, dear me! It has seemed mere minutes. But I have it, Mr Holmes; rest assured, I have it – and more, too.'

'More? What is that, Professor?'

His expression suddenly turned wary.

'It were better I do not tell you,' he replied. 'The fewer who know what I have found, the safer.'

'Then the sooner your secrets are in my brother's keeping, the more secure they will be. I could wire him to send a Queen's Messenger to fetch the papers. He might even be persuaded to come in person again.'

'I should prefer to take the details to London myself.' He beat his fist almost petulantly on his bed. 'How can I, though, with that additional threat hanging over me of being way-laid? I fear I am no subject for a disguise.'

In the weeks since his visit, Mycroft had reported, he had had inquiries made about Colonel Sebastian Moran. He had not been seen at his London apartment for many months, having told the head porter of the block that he would be abroad indefinitely. The man had had no idea of his destina-tion, and what he could remember seeing of the Colonel's baggage had given him no inkling.

Reconsidering my own suggestions, I said, 'A Queen's Messenger could be risky. They are totally reliable, but there is always the outside possibility of his chancing to be attacked for the political messages which his bag might contain. Mycroft would perhaps come, but, as a man who is well known never to travel anywhere much outside the West End of London, it might excite suspicion in interested quarters if he were to make his way to this obscure place a second time. All in all, I had better go myself.'

Moriarty raised his oscillating head questioningly.

'You need have no fears for your documents with me, Professor,' I assured him. 'I can travel disguised all the way – in more than one disguise, in fact. It will give me an opportunity to find out from Mycroft what his next plans will be, particularly as regards yourself. Meanwhile, you will be as safe as houses here.'

'It is a main part of your duty to protect me,' he reminded me.

'I shall depute that job to our worthy landlord.'

'Steiler? What use is he likely to be?'

'I have never told you, Professor, but Peter Steiler is an agent whom we can trust to the end of the game. All along, he has been one of the few who have known the truth about our joint "demise", and since our return here he has been keeping his eye out on behalf of both of us. With me temporarily absent, he will concentrate all his watchfulness on you.'

There would have been no point in adding the obvious – that while I was gone, Steiler's other task would be to ensure that Moriarty did not make it convenient to take his leave of Meiringen on his own account. With me out of the way with one copy of his notes – and how could I know whether they were the genuine ones, or a 'doctored' set? – he might well take it into his head to go off in quite another direction with the real things. Perhaps Moriarty did not miss the implication, though, for he gave me his rare, slow-spreading smile.

'An excellent arrangement, Mr Holmes. And you may rest assured that your journey will not be a wasted one. Your brother and his scientific advisers will be more than satisfied with what you bring them.'

So I travelled to London, in the successive guises of a stout Swiss businessman, moustached, bearded, and cigar-smoking; a French artist, in rough country clothes and carrying a knapsack from which brushes and palette protruded; and, for the Channel crossing, a wan English travelling salesman, professing exasperation with foreigners, and longing for reunion with 'the missus and little brats' in Manchester.

Moriarty had copied out all his working into one consolidated document, many pages long, consisting of copious formulae and notes. I insisted before leaving that he deliver all his working notes into Steiler's hands for concealment in a place of assured safety. Unless the Professor could carry it all in his head, elude Steiler's watch, and get away from the neighbourhood with his memory unimpaired, we were insured against his defection.

It was strange, returning to London after the best part of three years. Until this mission had come along it had been the centre of my own web, from where I radiated my strands of thought and conjecture. I travelled mentally to other places and into other situations described by the clients of both sexes and many walks of life who came to consult me, so that, as often as not, I was able to advise them without stirring from the congenial haven of 221B Baker Street.

The great metropolis appeared as bustling, dirty and noisy as ever, if not more so after the comparative cleanliness of Germany and Switzerland. It was the early winter of 1893, and the damp air retained the acid reek of recent fog and the clay exposed by the many street works which I found in progress as the face of the city underwent widespread changes.

While Mycroft's experts conferred urgently over Moriarty's notes he proposed to incarcerate me in the depths of the Diogenes Club where I should run no risk of recognition. I demurred absolutely, preferring to trust to the disguise of an old gentleman and lodging in a small hotel off the Strand. It left me free to saunter about the city, noting changes, great and small, which had taken place in it during my absence.

The most striking of these was the Tower Bridge, almost completed after nearly thirty years' work. At long last I was able to watch its centre span of roadway raised in two halves to allow vessels to pass; and I walked across its upper footway, enjoying a fine panoramic view of the sprawl of the metropolis.

The Imperial Institute in South Kensington, also finished at last, struck me as somewhat out of keeping, in its Renaissance bulk, with the British scene. More appealing to my eye as a work

My incognito visit to London late in 1893 enabled me to see Tower
Bridge almost completed at last after nearly thirty years' work.
I viewed the panorama from the upper footway and watched
the roadway beneath raised to allow vessels to pass.

by the same architect, T. E. Colcutt, was the pretty, concave-
fronted playhouse at Cambridge Circus, where Shaftesbury
Avenue meets the Charing Cross Road. Alas for cultural aspirations, I found a fall here. When it had been opened, 'regardless
of expense', by D'Oyly Carte shortly before my enforced exile,

The Royal English Opera House, at Cambridge Circus, had been opened shortly before my exile by Richard D'Oyly Carte for the performance of indigenous works. Sullivan's IVANHOE *had a mixed reception, though, and with few other works available the theatre became a variety house, The Palace.*

it had been as the Royal English Opera House, intended to herald the rebirth of serious indigenous music and give it a permanent home. I had attended the first presentation there, Sullivan's only grand opera, *Ivanhoe*, but, like many others, had come away mourning the absence of that sparkle which so distinguished his work with Gilbert. In my absence it had been sold and turned into a variety theatre, the Palace, which is its own commentary on our British taste; though who could blame anyone who preferred the inspired absurdities of Dan Leno, Albert Chevalier, Lottie Collins, Ada Reeve, Vesta Tilley and

Charles Coburn to a studious blending of Sir Walter Scott with Arthur Sullivan at his most earnest?

In Piccadilly Circus, that hub of the British Empire, I found an amusing novelty. During my absence, in 1893, there had been erected a fountain incorporating what was claimed to be the world's largest aluminium statue, depicting a naked, winged and helmeted figure of a boy discharging a bow, in personification of charity flying to the rescue. He has since become familiar the world over as Eros.

The sculpture had been created by Sir Alfred Gilbert as a memorial to that most worthy philanthropist Lord Shaftesbury, who had died in 1885, but the figure's lack of clothing had attracted many censorious comments. I was told that some respectable families found it preferable to make a detour of Piccadilly Circus or to avert their eyes in passing the spot.

A stroll along Baker Street was scarcely to be resisted; but the impulse to enter the old premises and receive Mrs Hudson's tearful welcome, to spend a blessed hour in the fireside chair with all the familiar impedimenta about me, to inquire after Watson, his bereavement, and any news which the good lady would have had for me of his health and spirits and whereabouts – that was the strongest temptation of all, and needed the most firm resistance, and I forbade myself to go that way.

After only two days of this freedom, I received at my hotel the letter by hand which, purporting to come from the London Library whose name its envelope bore, was my expected summons to the Diogenes Club. Mycroft himself met me in the lobby and led me away, quite cutting out the morose porter's interrogation.

Mycroft's own expression was serious as he turned from locking the Committee Room door.

'You look troubled,' I observed, seating myself and stroking my false whiskers. 'Can't they understand his findings?'

'Far from it,' he answered sombrely, proceeding to pour us both some coffee from a silver jug. 'They are a model of clarity – a wonder to behold, they say.'

'Then? You don't say they don't add up to anything?'

'Wrong again, I'm afraid. In terms of pure mathematics the exercise is immaculate. He has worked out the entire theoretical basis of what the Germans have been seeking to do. He has gone even further than that.'

'He said there was something extra.'

'He has found that the wavelengths of the radio waves envisaged by the Germans for this purpose are one metre or so in length, in a continuous emission, but that the nature of the equipment would result in making them considerably longer than that, which would result in an even feebler signal. Moriarty's notion is that what is needed instead is a series of short pulses of radiation, using very short wavelengths – millimetres or centimetres, rather than metres. This would make not only for greater power, but would, as it were, bounce back a regular stream of echoes from the target, indicating the direction and speed in which it is travelling. The directional transmitter could therefore follow it, no matter how it might change course. It would be caught as though in the full beam of a searchlight, yet without knowing it. It could not escape, and it would be a simple matter to fire a gun or a torpedo along the same lines as the echoing beam. There is even a footnote to say that there is no reason why the beam could not be directed downward into the sea, to pinpoint the position of a hidden submarine. Apparently it will work as well through water as darkness, fog or the clearest air.'

I so far forgot my surroundings as to whistle.

'It is the ultimate weapon both of defence and attack, then.'

'Precisely.' Mycroft fixed me with sorrowful, almost pleading eyes. 'The only snag is, it won't work.'

'Won't work!'

'Can't, rather. As I said, Moriarty's theory, brilliant and entirely feasible as it is, exists only in mathematical form. The technical equipment needed to put it into practice *does not exist*. Without it, the whole concept is useless.'

A QUESTION OF EXPEDIENCY

'Useless!' I echoed, striving to digest all the implications of his announcement. 'Do you mean to tell me that I have devoted almost three years of the prime of my life and career – I say nothing of Professor Moriarty's – in working towards what you are telling me is a complete but useless achievement?'

'Now you are exaggerating the position, Sherlock,' Mycroft scolded. 'The basis of all intelligence work is the principle of "need to know". If you will simmer down and review the situation, you will recognize that, while admittedly negative rather than positive where we are concerned, it is an entirely satisfactory one nevertheless. At least we know where we stand *via-à-vis* Germany and the other nations. So far as the theory goes, we have the sum total of the equation showing how electromagnetic waves may be used to detect, identify, follow and lead to the destruction of hostile vessels, on or under the sea. For all we know, our rivals have not yet got even that far; they are probably still struggling with their formulae. The great pity as I say, is that the theory cannot be translated into a practical system. There is no equipment capable of the task.'

'Do you mean here, or anywhere?'

'Anywhere. That is why I describe the situation as satisfactory. If we cannot do it, with the complete theory at our disposal, no one else can. Great Britain is not a belligerent power. Our whole desire is peace. So long as we know that we are abreast, and preferably ahead, of those from whom hostilities might be anticipated, we are content.'

'That has a slightly smug ring to me, Mycroft. If we go on thinking like that for ever, we might come to regret it.

'How so?'

'Well, supposing the Germans, or French, or whoever, had reached this solution first, or developed any other warlike system you care to mention before we could match it, we could be taken unawares. Supposing, for example, Moriarty actually had defected to one of them with his completed equation.'

'I tell you, it would make no difference. You cannot advance practical science by thirty, forty, fifty years on the strength of a perfect theory. Small electrical signals *cannot* be amplified; there is no device capable of producing the short wavelength emissions which the system requires; the only apparatus for receiving an image or a reflected impulse is the photographic plate, which would be useless in this instance.'

'Surely the perfection of the theory will lead swiftly to the necessary developments?'

'No, Sherlock. Even a mathematical genius such as Moriarty cannot show how to compress years of technical innovation into a short period. We are back to Leonardo da Vinci and his theory of flight. Man still has not mastered the practicalities of it.'

I sank against the back of the upright chair at the table of that committee room. The door was locked, but no one had so much as turned the knob to try to enter. Come to that, I could not envisage the committee of the Diogenes Club ever meeting; its members would be virtual strangers, and what business they might have to discuss beggared the imagination. Yet, our business concerned international security, even dominance, and there seemed to be nothing more to be said about that, either.

One thing did occur to me, though.

'What is the next step, Mycroft?'

'Naturally, the scientists and physicists will go to work on the problems. There is nothing so potent as a known objective for concentrating endeavours.'

'And while they are about it, I expect some agent or traitor or suborned official will lay hands on the formulae, so that by the time we reach the goal the others will have caught up with us.'

'That is uncalled for, Sherlock. It is well known that our security is second to none.'

'I could instance you one major threat to it here and now.'

'What is that?'

'Moriarty.'

'Moriarty? What has he to do with it?'

'It merely happens to be his brainchild. Have you considered what his reaction will be when you tell him that it will have to be aborted?'

From Mycroft's expression I could tell that he had thought no such thing.

'He . . . he will understand,' he faltered, his tone carrying not the least conviction.

'No, Mycroft, he will not understand. As you have so often reminded me, he is a theoretician. He has fulfilled his task of proving that a certain thing is capable of achievement. Is he now to be told that it is not, after all, because no one possesses, or has the ingenuity to construct, the required bits and pieces of apparatus? I know what I should do in his place, given his cast of mind.'

'What is that?'

'Erupt. Go berserk.'

'Well, I am sorry about that – sorry for our own sake, never mind his; but there is nothing we can do about it.'

'There has to be something. It is vital. Put yourself in his place, Mycroft. His legitimate career is null and void. We have killed him off, in the world's eyes; condemned him to a pseudonymous identity, under which he can make no claims on behalf of his past achievements. Suppose some bright new theoretician comes up tomorrow with work in the field of the binomial theorem or the dynamics of an asteroid? He will naturally make passing – possibly dismissive – reference to the early but misguided work of the late Professor James Moriarty, then go on to reconstruct it to his own conception. Imagine Moriarty having to look helplessly on while a new man receives the plaudits he was denied, while he himself is pushed deeper into obscurity in the process.'

'Uncomfortable, I agree; but, as I told you before, his work on the asteroid is flawed. His results are ones he wanted to reach, but he got them only by conveniently by-passing obstacles which he could not legitimately remove. Therefore, he has no genuine grounds for complaint.'

'That counts for nothing in Moriarty's mind. He convinced himself, and that is all that matters to him. Anyone who will not acknowledge that he is right is at best an incompetent and at worst an enemy. And now, in this present instance, he will find us readily acknowledging that he is right, but professing to be unable to make use of his discoveries. Can't you see what a head of frustration that is going to bring him to?'

Mycroft shrugged resignedly. 'He will have to be persuaded of the plain truth. We can acknowledge our long-term debt to him, but insist that we are powerless to do anything until much practical research has been conducted.'

I shook my head. 'I know this man. He will feel certain that either our people are incompetents, or that we are up to the old tricks which have so seared him in the past. We have got his results, we are perfectly capable of putting them to use, but we don't wish to acknowledge him.'

'But why on earth should we take that attitude? The work is secret. It will not be published, so there is no question of public acknowledgment and, in any case, he will be Etherage, or any other name he chooses except Moriarty, for the rest of his life, which makes recognition meaningless anyway.

'Mycroft, you will insist on ascribing sweet reason to his mentality. The man is a paranoiac. If you want my opinion, I believe he will take his findings straight to the Germans.'

'The Germans!'

'It is his most logical course. He has served us, and has made a great discovery in doing so. But, either from duplicity or incompetence, we are proposing to do nothing about it. "Well done, Professor. Good day to you." Where should you go after such a brush-off as that?'

'One thing is definite,' Mycroft said grimly; 'he is not going to the Germans.'

'The French, then. The Russians. He has proved an immaculate theory – without any recourse to wishful thinking this time. He is not a young man. The one ambition left to him is to see himself vindicated, even anonymously. I do not think that, in the long run, it will matter to him who accords him that recognition, so long as he gets it.'

'Dear me, Sherlock, this is tiresome of you,' grumbled Mycroft, easing his bulk in his chair. 'Just when everything had worked out so neatly.'

'Don't blame me, or you will have me turning paranoid too. Tell me, by the way, what future plans *have* you in mind for the Professor?'

Mycroft fidgeted again, and I detected a disturbing furtiveness about him.

'We, er, are not wholly decided. There are a number of problems about that.'

'I'm sure there are. For example, where is he to live? As you have said, scarcely in England. You cannot expect him to spend the rest of his days shut away from life.'

'It has always been assumed that he would be happier living abroad, for the sake of his own freedom of movement as much as for our convenience.'

'Living abroad, eh? With a secret in his possession for which any major power would set him up in state and proclaim his name throughout the scientific world. His *real* name, mark you. Think what jolly mischief the French or Germans could create by making public what really happened at Reichenbach, and how the unwilling tool of a blackmailing British Government outwitted it, and came to them in the final event.'

The sharp slap of Mycroft's heavy palm, brought down flat on the table top, made me jump.

'Stop it, Sherlock! This is no crowing matter. Don't you think my mind has been full of these problems which you toss off so airily? Professor Moriarty's future is a considerable worry to me, from any point of view.'

I looked hard at my brother. I had no illusions about his capacity for ruthlessness in his conduct of his clandestine trade. He was not a naturally cruel man, nor an unfeeling one. So far as scruples and the decencies could be conveniently observed he would observe them; but faced with a situation where they became a hindrance or a threat, he would not hesitate to trample over them.

As he observed, I had been teasing him about Moriarty. It had always been a pleasure of mine to argue him into a corner, if only for the pleasure of watching him spar his way out of it. It was a mutually enjoyable tussle; only, this time, it had suddenly ceased to amuse me. It was not I who had cornered him on this occasion; circumstances had done it already, and all his trick ways of getting out were blocked. The remaining alternatives were drastic and grim. The helpless, apologetic way he returned my stare told me all.

'Not that, Mycroft,' I urged.

He gazed at me bleakly. 'It seems not long ago that you were saying you would do anything to bring about that man's destruction, Sherlock.'

'It was three years ago. I have come to know him since. I will not go so far as to say that I have come to like him. Say, rather, that I have come to recognize the way in which any of us, given changed circumstances, could have turned out to be other than what we are.'

'My present circumstances, Sherlock – and I speak not on my own behalf, but for Her Majesty's Government – are that we have here a man of brilliant but unstable mind and intense criminal tendencies. He has in his possession a secret of great magnitude and of his personal discovery, which he is soon to be told is of no immediate use to us, but probably will be in due course, by which time he may well be dead of old age. As you observe, it is extremely unlikely that he will accept this to be the truth, with the consequence that, as almost any other ambitious, impatient, abnormally self-centred man would, he will consider where else he might hope to find better under-standing and a fulfilment which he believes us incapable or unwilling to give him. The nature of his secret renders us un-able to countenance any such action by him. If you have any alternative suggestion for resolving my dilemma, Sherlock, other than locking him up and throwing away the key, or – but the only one remaining I prefer not to put into words – then for Heaven's sake let me hear it.'

'Very well,' I replied. 'Here it is.'

A Naval Occasion

THE GOVERNOR of Her Majesty's Prison at Portland, in Dorsetshire, had been ordered to cancel all outdoor working parties for that one day. It occurred to me that the convicts would not be sorry to be deprived of their fresh air and exercise, the latter consisting of breaking limestone in the cement quarries. It was December, and the winds which swept the craggy peninsula were keen-edged enough to make a man feel he was being sliced in two.

The Home Office had given the Governor no explanation, save that a secret naval exercise was due to take place in Weymouth Bay, and that there would be high-ranking officers and others observing from the vantage point of Henry VIII's old castle. The precaution was perhaps excessive: none of the enforced labourers among the white stone slabs would have recognized Professor Moriarty. Not even those who were there because of him knew him by sight.

There were a few of the old lags, however, who might have stared at the apparent shade of Sherlock Holmes among them. It had been thought prudent to keep them indoors, even though I was wearing the uniform of a Commander R.N. and sporting a fine naval beard, a combination which I must admit to thinking not unflattering to my appearance.

No attempt was made to disguise Moriarty; it would have been hopeless. He wore a black soft hat, well pulled down around the brim, and kept his coat's astrakhan collar well up about his chin, as much for protection against the cold as for concealment.

Against his physical inclinations, Mycroft had grudgingly accepted that he, too, must attend. The rest of our small party were naval officers and a handful of Whitehall civilians, posing as scientists. Genuine ones had to be excluded, for fear one of them might chance to recognize Moriarty.

The limestone quarries at Portland, Dorset, were worked largely by convicts from the prison. This bleak site, overlooking the great naval base and Weymouth Bay, was chosen for the demonstration of the location of warships by radio waves, which had a dramatically unexpected climax.

The vast, deepwater Portland Harbour, whose breakwaters were at that time still under construction by convicts to make it almost the equivalent area of the semi-island itself, was thronged with craft of all shapes and sizes, from the biggest new screw-driven ironclads to the paddle-wheeled men-o'-war which they were rapidly rendering obsolete, and many steam-and-sail and sail-only vessels. Further out, in Weymouth Bay itself, three warships alone were visible through the glasses with which we had come equipped. They were described respectively to us laymen as a battle-cruiser, a coastal defence monitor, of much shallower draught and lying low in the water, and, the smallest, a torpedo gunboat.

We were conducted to a wooden hut, in the lee of one of the highest rocky pinnacles. Its windows afforded a panoramic view of Weymouth Bay, to as far east as St Aldhelm's Head, with the Dorset coastline gleaming between on what was a clear, sunny day. It made an impressive vista; but all our immediate attention was concentrated upon the contents of the hut in which we gathered, leaving a guard of sailors standing to attention all around outside.

From what little I had seen of that laboratory in Karlsruhe, I recognized this to be a fair representation of it. There was little in the way of furniture, apart from some benches and a table, on which was spread a large canvas chart, delineating the bay before us. Little wooden models had been made of the three naval vessels out there, and were lying on the table beside the chart.

Under the window was a bench, equipped with small items of gadgetry, and behind that, horizontal against the wall, was a black panel, into which were set dials of varying size. There was much wiring in evidence, disappearing below the bench into boxes and Leyden jars, and up through the hut roof, above which we had seen before entering a piece of apparatus roughly resembling a weather vane atop a metal pole. It was not swinging in the wind, however, but lay rigid, only vibrating from the forceful strength of the blast which swept over this barren place.

A Chief Petty Officer, bearing many badges of proficiency, stood stiffly to attention from his seat at this control panel, while another stood beside a wheel, whose obvious purpose was to rotate the vane on the roof.

An officer more resplendent than the rest in gold braid, gold leaf on his hat, several rows of medals, and the star of an Imperial Order, invited all of us to be seated, except the Petty Officers, who stood stiffly at ease behind him as he addressed us.

'Gentlemen, I propose to be brief in my introduction to this demonstration. Each one of us knows already what its purpose is: to test for the first time outside the laboratory the electromagnetic range-finding apparatus which has been built according to the principles arrived at by Professor Etherage, who is among our number today. Quite simply, the object of the

181

The breakwater of Portland naval base was still being built by convicts at the time of the demonstration. A battle-cruiser, a monitor and a torpedo gunboat were the 'targets' for the electromagnetic range-finding apparatus derived from the theories of Clerk Maxwell, Hertz and 'Etherage'.

exercise is to try to locate in turn each of the three warships at present lying in Weymouth Bay by directional beam from the antenna on the roof of this hut and the corresponding echo which, if all proceeds smoothly, will be received back from the target.'

'I can see them with my naked eyes,' drawled one of the civilians, raising a general chuckle.

The officer in charge of the proceedings smiled and gave a slight indication to the Chief Petty Officer at the panel, who turned about smartly and reached for the pull of a dark canvas blind which he drew down over the window. At the same time he pressed one of his many switches and the room was illuminated by a single light bulb.

'I can still see them,' the civilian persisted. 'That is to say, I could place them for you from memory, in relation to features of the coastline.'

Heinrich Hertz's oscillator. The terminals of an induction coil (bottom left) were connected to a condenser, A-B, causing a spark to travel between the two brass balls, a-b, thus forming a path for subsequent oscillations, which were measured.

'That objection has been anticipated, Sir George,' said the officer smoothly. He addressed a naval rating, who had followed us in unnoticed and stood with his back to the door.

'Signaller.'

'Sir!' The man sprang to attention.

'Go outside and make to the ships to commence steaming.'

'Aye aye, sir.'

The man went out, closing the door. The officer resumed.

'The captains have been awaiting a heliograph signal from here to begin steaming. They may go wherever they wish in the entire bay which has been specially kept clear for them. They have been given thirty minutes, at the end of which they will have dispersed too widely for any of us to guess where each will be. Only then will the test begin.'

The minutes passed slowly. A number of questions about the apparatus were put, but beyond reiterating its general principles the officer would give no details.

'I am sorry, gentlemen, but you will appreciate that the technical details must remain a complete secret to all except the three gentlemen whose dedicated labour has brought this apparatus into being, based on Professor Etherage's theoretical findings. Without the Professor's brilliant vision and formidable mathematics – which I am the first to admit to a complete inability to understand – none of this would have been possible. However, I feel sure that the Professor himself would wish to join us in tribute to the skill of the scientists in transforming theory into reality. I understand – and I venture to say it deepens my admiration for him a thousandfold – that his results were arrived at wholly in mathematical terms, without any knowledge whatever of the nature of the equipment needed to make his concept work.'

This produced a warm round of applause and murmurs of admiration. Moriarty poked out his pale face, tortoise-like, and smiled thinly from side to side, before withdrawing again into his upturned collar.

'Fortunately for us,' the officer continued, 'most of the equipment did exist, or could be modified from other items. I will make no secret that a number of the components in the apparatus had to be developed specially and are therefore unique, and it is my duty to charge every one of you to reveal nothing of what occurs here today. The scientists themselves are under strict orders to answer no questions, put formally or otherwise, and Professor Etherage has indicated that he has no statement to make, whatever the outcome of the trials.'

An elderly uniformed officer cleared his throat and spoke up.

'Captain, I must insist on asking one question before the proceedings begin, and I believe I am not going too far in demanding a categorical answer.'

'Please put your question, Admiral,' replied the other, with a wary look.

'It is this. I require to know whether there is the slightest hazard to those ships or the people in them from being subjected to these rays?'

The conducting officer looked clearly relieved.

'I give you that undertaking categorically, Admiral,' he answered. 'The scientists will confirm it?'

Three younger men in civilian clothes, seated side by side, nodded in silent unison.

'Thank you,' the Admiral said, and resumed his silence.

The Chief Petty Officer now spoke up.

'With permission, sir, thirty minutes elapsed exactly.'

'Very well, Chief. Switch on.'

'Aye aye, sir.'

The C.P.O. seated himself at his panel, his back to the rest of us, and pressed three switches. The air was immediately filled with the hum of electricity. Needles on the gauges in his panel sprang to life and began flickering to and fro. As one man, we leaned forward on our seats, our eyes focused on the man at the controls. One tattooed hand grasped a lever, which appeared capable of sliding to and fro in a horizontal groove, about twelve inches in length. The other held a similar lever on the opposite side of the panel, whose movements within its channel would be vertical, up or down.

Without turning his head he rapped out an order.

'Stand to the antenna.'

'Aye aye, Chief,' came from the other Petty Officer, who in turn became the object of our attention as he grasped the wheel which was his charge.

'Hard aport,' from the C.P.O.

'Hard aport, Chief.' The wheelsman turned the wheel smartly to the left as far as it would go. 'Full port, Chief.'

'Begin traversing.'

185

'Traversing, Chief.'

Every breath was held as the wheel began to be turned back to the right, a fraction of an inch at a time. It moved slowly, but smoothly, without pausing, while at the same time the Chief Petty Officer worked his two levers, horizontal and vertical, evidently seeking that point of coincidence where the beam from the slowly revolving antenna on the roof would strike one of the vessels which lay in the bay and be reflected back by its iron hull.

The needles flickered, the electricity hummed, with an occasional sparking crackle somewhere out of sight. For minutes nothing happened. Then, suddenly, we all jumped in our seats as a sharp ping sounded from within the control panel.

'Target located, sir,' shouted the C.P.O.

'Steady as she goes!' ordered the Captain excitedly.

The wheelsman repeated it and stopped turning. The two levers on the console were now the keys to the action, as the operator moved them gradually through their possible permutations.

There came the pinging sound again. It continued to sound at several seconds' interval. In a short while it became distinctly fainter, then was silenced altogether.

'Port!' rapped the C.P.O. at the wheelsman, who had not left hold of his charge, not even to brush away the perspiration of concentration which was trickling copiously down his neck.

He turned the wheel to port, as slowly as before, the C.P.O. making no adjustment to his controls, only waiting. After a moment or two he countermanded his order: 'Starboard. Starboard!'

His junior colleague turned the wheel back the other way, slightly more quickly. Within a few seconds he was rewarded by another faint ping, followed by a loud one as he turned the wheel further.

'Keep going, Jock!' ordered the C.P.O., forgetting protocol, and the wheelsman obeyed. By turning the wheel steadily to starboard he kept the console bell pinging.

The Captain in charge turned to us all: 'You hear, gentlemen! The target has been located by the beam. It was lost again, when it moved out of the beam's path. The operator ordered a sweep first to port, to ascertain whether that was the way it had gone. Failure to pick up the echo within a few seconds told him his error, and a quick adjustment to starboard relocated it. As you can hear, the target is still within the beam, which is following it. Signaller.'

'Sir?'

'Make to all ships to anchor.'

'Aye aye, sir.'

The Signaller hurried out once more. The Captain turned to his audience, forgetful enough of his dignity and the momentousness of the occasion to smile broadly as he said, 'That concludes the first phase of the demonstration. One of the vessels has been located by the electromagnetic beam. It was lost again briefly, as it moved out of the beam's path, but picked up within less than a minute by rotation of the antenna. As you can hear, the signal is inescapably locked on to the ship, and would remain so for a precise bearing to be taken and, if desired, fire to be opened on it.'

Great excitement prevailed, and there was even applause. The pinging rang out at monotonous intervals in the background. The Captain motioned to the operator to switch off its sound while he spoke again.

'The three vessels are now at anchor. By rotating the antenna further we shall locate the other two. The positions of all three, as ascertained by the apparatus, will be charted and compared afterwards with readings taken by conventional visual range-finder. As extra confirmation, the ships' captains have been ordered to record their own positions on anchoring. When all three records are compared, gentlemen, I think it will emerge that each reading coincides.'

The Chief Petty Officer handed him a slip of paper, bearing the readings indicated by the final position of his sliding controls. The Captain moved to the chart on the table.

'Which of the vessels has been located thus far remains to be seen. I will take the liberty of placing the model of the battle-cruiser on the spot first indicated. The test will continue with the vessels remaining at anchor, establishing first of all the positions of the other two, and then, by comparison of the strengths of the respective reflected signals, to attempt to ascertain which of them is which. Carry on, Chief.'

'Aye aye, sir.'

The controls were reactivated. As the antenna was inched round by its wheel control the familiar pinging noises rang out on two more occasions, indicating fixes on the positions of the remaining two vessels. There was detectable a distinct variation in the strength of the three echoes, enabling the Captain to place the respective models on their bearings. With excitement high among the naval and civilian personnel, we tumbled out of the hut and, sure enough, saw the scattered ships exactly where we had been told each would be.

Congratulations reigned all round, and several men came up to Moriarty, insistent upon shaking his hand. He smiled back wanly, but would only murmur his thanks, refusing to be drawn into any conversation.

I found myself left alone at his side. He turned his oscillating gaze upon me and remained thus for some moments, before wandering slowly across the white rocky surface to where it fell away steeply. I kept up with him. The hearty voices of the others, exulting in the morning's success, were wafted to us on the blustery wind.

Moriarty stopped, and turned to look at me.

'It is unworthy of you, Mr Holmes,' he said.

'I . . . I beg your pardon, Professor?'

'Or, no doubt, I should say of your brother – for I have no doubt that he is behind it, though you have doubtless been in on the secret all along.'

'Secret? I have been with you in Meiringen these past few months while we have been waiting for the apparatus to be developed, and I have received no more information about it than yourself.'

This was literally true. I had gone back there from my conference with Mycroft, carrying assurances to Moriarty that the work was being put in hand at once, and that we were to remain in the safety of our retreat until word came that tests had been successfully carried out under laboratory conditions. Only then should we risk the journey to England to witness the actual demonstration among representatives of the Admiralty and the Royal Navy.

Moriarty's gaze held mine though, and I could see appearing deep in his eyes the glitter of anger. The tone of his voice sharpened correspondingly.

'If you have been truly taken in by the charade which has just been staged for my benefit, then you are as big a fool as the rest of them. That is, unless every one of them is in the plot against me. I would not put that past that brother of yours, but old instinct shows me your own hand in this.'

He was, of course, quite right. The whole thing had been my idea; but I had found myself so gripped by the excitement of it, and the convincing way in which it had been set up and carried out, none of which I had known in advance, that I had quite forgotten that the demonstration had been a fake on the grand scale which it was well within Mycroft's power to order. I found myself defending it with the firmness of self-delusion.

'Come now, Professor. Against you? Why should anyone be against you? There isn't a man here today who wouldn't wish to congratulate and praise you personally, if you would accept it. When the system is perfected and adopted operationally it will bear your name – as Etherage, I mean. You are certain to be handsomely rewarded and, I expect, honoured by the government for your contribution to your country's defence. . . .'

'Oh yes. All that – and why? To ensure my silence. To remove me from the scene, so that my ideas may be conveniently put on some shelf by fools who either cannot make them reality or, even more likely, have not the slightest intention of trying. It is enough for them to have used me to find out what the Germans were doing. Having discovered that there was nothing to fear from that quarter, the problem of disposing of me remains. It would not be British to do so by violent means, yet I may not be trusted to remain at large. Then there is your own precious career to consider. Instead of having to go on hiding away as my watchdog, you need to be enabled to make some miraculous return to the land of the living and carry on with your interfering work, while I am condemned to live out a shadow life.'

He had stated the matter so accurately, and recognized his fate so clearly, that I felt impelled to confide in him, even at some cost to the truth.

'Professor, I admit that today's exhibition was to a large extent faked. It was, if you like, a demonstration to those officials of what your system will be capable when it is developed – a means to persuade them to provide the money and facilities to enable the development to go forward. You must believe me when I give you my word that certain of the vital technical knowledge does not yet exist to enable it to work. Rather than risk your assuming, as you have done, that the

will to pursue it is absent, it was thought worth inviting you to be present in the hope that you would feel as satisfied as the rest of them.'

'By a bungling affair like that!'

'I thought it entirely convincing!'

Moriarty snorted. 'You think me a mere theoretician – a conjuror with symbols and formulae which you cannot understand. It was not by chalking figures on a blackboard that I put together an empire of crime which has probably never had its equal in history. It was through foresight, perception, cunning. I, too, have played tricks on gullible onlookers. Unlike you, however, I have known where to draw the line; where deception has its limits, and absurdity shows through. This demonstration was effective enough up to a point – locating the ships and confirming that they lay precisely where that bogus business with ringing bells and switches and dials located them. Had it been left at that, even I might have accepted it. But to ask one to believe that the differing sizes of vessels could be ascertained by the strength or faintness of a mere echo – dear me, Mr Holmes, dear me! An echo from a metal object can be nothing more than that. The object's size, relative to the signal's strength, is irrelevant.'

The anger had faded from his eyes. I saw reproach and disenchantment in its place. I also saw miserably how right he was. Excess of zeal in the preparations had overlooked so simple a truth.

'It was part of your theory that the size of targets could be ascertained by the radio waves,' I reminded him.

'Yes – in time. But even I did not suppose that such sophisticated development could be hoped for without entirely new equipment – whole systems and functions which have probably not been conceived so far, and might not be for years to come. I am a *theoretician*, Mr Holmes. I project the future. Then it is for the mere mechanics, the artisans, to catch up with me. I will give you one more prediction for my system which I have not yet even formulated, because it is so inconceivable in the light of present-day physics. It is . . .'

He spoke no further. With a sudden look of startled surprise on his face he staggered forward against me. I tried to seize him, but was too late. He slid down my body and legs, to lie crumpled and still at my feet.

Munich Revisited

For a moment I believed he had suffered an apoplexy. One of the others had seen him fall, and shouted to the rest. The whole group came running. By the time they reached us, I had found that he had been shot.

There had been no gun report. The bullet, which had struck him squarely in the back, beneath the left shoulder blade, had left a small, clean entry hole, indicating a high velocity shot from quite some distance. The bullet had not emerged from his chest. It was almost certainly soft-nosed, then, and had expanded inside him, causing a mortal wound.

A soft-nosed bullet; high velocity; no sound; the victim Moriarty . . . I seized Mycroft by the arm and pulled him down, to say close to his ear, 'Shot. Moran, for a certainty. Get the navy people searching – but no names.'

He nodded, and hurried away to the Captain, who soon sent the sentries off in all directions, with their rifles and bayonets at the ready.

There was no one with medical qualifications among our group. From the look of Moriarty, and the nature of the wound, I had no doubt that he was within minutes of death. It would have been pointless to take him to one of the horse carriages which awaited us on the road some hundred yards away. He would be dead before we could even get him into one.

He groaned. I leaned down to him, and cradled his head. Even now, its oscillating continued, but it was a more painful movement, and blood trickled from a corner of his mouth.

He opened his eyes into slits, and recognized me. I saw that he was trying to speak, and with a gesture I indicated to Mycroft to keep the others back, ostensibly to give air, but actually for fear that the dying man might say something which we would prefer not to be overheard.

'Am . . . am I shot?' he gasped.

'Professor,' I said urgently. 'I swear it was none of our doing. Believe that. I'm sure it was Moran.'

He managed a faint nod of acknowledgment.

'Was . . . going . . . keep faith. Queen and Country, Mr . . . Mr Fisher.'

'I shall get him, I promise you. I'll find him somehow.'

He nodded again. With my handkerchief I dabbed at the blood on his lips, but it continued to trickle out. His chest was heaving now, with the effort to draw breath.

'Professor,' I said. 'One more prediction, you were saying. Is it important? What were you going to say?'

The effort to speak again was almost beyond him. I feared I should hear no more. But between the harsh rasping sounds of his last breaths, he sighed, rather than spoke: 'Over . . . horizon. Beam. Detect . . . over horizon. Must be . . . feasible. Tell them . . . keep trying. Keep on. . . .'

His voice trailed away. There came a gush of blood, and he was dead.

Mycroft took charge from that point. He moved in mysterious ways, and his power was so widespread that no newspaper carried any report of a shooting at Portland. All who had been present, including the naval ratings, were specially sworn to silence about everything which had occurred.

Neither sight nor trace of Moran was found. The police were not notified. There was no inquest. Since 'Professor Etherage' appeared, according to Mycroft's account, to have neither kith nor kin living, it was agreed that, having been engaged at the time of his death on work associated with the Admiralty and the Royal Navy, he should be accorded the honour of burial at sea from one of H.M. warships.

Still in my naval uniform, I was present at the simple ceremony, out on the waters of Weymouth Bay. It was as moving as all Service burials are, especially those at sea, where the body is committed to the cleansing, ever-living waters, rather than the austere confines of the grave.

As I stood in my place, at the destroyer's stern, listening to the beautiful old words read out by the chaplain, and the bugle's silver notes, and watched the weighted canvas bundle slide into the depths, I thought how much of my own life had been bound up with his, in both antagonism and collaboration. Human nature, I reflected, is a strange mixture, when even a villain, a blackmailer, a wrecker of lives, and an instigator of murder can inspire affection in his most dedicated opponent. I had gained some insight into his complex nature, and witnessed his potential for good, and had watched retribution come to him, not as a result of justified and lawful condemnation, but at the hand of a scoundrel acting from no higher motive than his own revenge. In that moment I could genuinely mourn Professor James Moriarty.

I swore to myself, furthermore, that before resuming my own career I would honour my promise to him, and find and pay out Colonel Sebastian Moran, even if it meant postponing for a further period my increasingly longed-for return to my old identity and way of life.

The bullet fragments assembled after the autopsy, which I attended, left no doubt that he had been killed with a soft-nosed revolver bullet. Moran's air-rifle was adapted to fire such a projectile, and silently. A single shot from a place of concealment in that rocky area had been enough; and Moran was a crack-shot. No tell-tale sound had indicated his whereabouts. He had been able to make his escape along the causeway to the mainland before the guards could come looking for him.

The other fact which made this plain to me – and it was a not uncomforting one – was that Moran had not recognized me; otherwise there would have been two shots and two dead men on Mycroft's organizational hands. Apart from a certain grief on my behalf, as his brother, it should not have given him too many problems, however, for both Moriarty and I had officially been dead men for almost three years.

I could be thankful for having kept up my naval disguise on that day. Moran must certainly have known me by sight when he was working with Moriarty. Moriarty had for long feared that Moran suspected he still lived, and was on his trail; but that did not necessarily imply that he thought I was alive, too. More likely, he believed that Moriarty, having killed me at Reichenbach, had thought it expedient to disappear, and leave his London henchmen to face their own music, Moran included.

There were two immediate puzzles for me: where was Moran now? And how had he got onto Moriarty's trail?

I decided to tackle them in reverse order. Wherever Moran was, trying to find him would be like looking for a needle in a haystack. He was apparently unaware of my survival, and had come and gone at Portland unseen and unsuspected, so he need take no special precautions which would involve going into hiding.

All the same, seasoned villain as he was, he would lie low for some time, watching for any newspaper reports of the shooting. I thought I could leave Moran to his own devices, letting him get back the full confidence which would embolden him to resume his normal ways once more, having left him completely off his guard.

As to the other matter, I had one valuable clue to go upon. When Moriarty's dead body had been borne away at last to one of those waiting carriages, for discreet transportation to the Royal Naval mortuary at the Portland base, his silver-headed cane had not accompanied it. That had remained in my possession; and a week later it was swinging jauntily in the hand of a grey-haired and moustached English gentleman in tweeds, who strode along the platform at Victoria to take his place in a first-class compartment on the boat train, which would bear him on the first leg of his journey to Munich. If anyone on the journey had asked him, companionably or from more pointed curiosity, why he was going there, he would have answered that he was a musicologist, going to spend some time immersed in the Bavarian state musical archives. In the event, no one asked; and, so far as I could judge, no one gave a second glance at my handsome cane.

At Munich I booked into a hotel convenient for the Bayerische Staatsbibliothek. Late in the afternoon I sallied forth and went straight to the little street where von Herder's workshop was situated.

I watched for a time, but saw no one coming or going, so went to the door and entered. As before, the old man was working alone, polishing with a loving caress the blue-black barrel of a rifle.

He came to his little counter with a polite greeting. I said nothing, leaving the opaque eyes to stare sightlessly at me for some moments. Then I reached forward and took hold of one of his hands in mine. Its back was wrinkled and veined with age, but the palm was silky-soft.

I shook the hand formally, then transferred it to the head of the cane. The fingers had barely touched the silver lion's head before there came the start of recognition, and a smile of greeting.

'Herr . . . Etherage!' the old man exclaimed, and I noticed that he swallowed hard after saying it.

'No,' I said in German, startling him considerably. 'Herr Etherage regrets he is unable to come. He has sent his, er, cane, as a token of recognition.'

The Market Square of Munich, with the Rathaus (town hall) on the right. Not visible in this view, a few hundred yards beyond the Rathaus, is the small street where the blind gunsmith von Herder had his workshop and made Col. Sebastian Moran's lethal air-rifle.

The old man stood still. I had no doubt that he had certain procedures in readiness for dealing with any sort of trouble which might visit a blind man, alone in a workshop, and especially one whose trade must attract more than a share of customers whose affairs were conducted away from the light of the law. He made no move, though, but stood waiting.

'I come as a friend of Herr Etherage,' I said.

'You have been here before,' he answered. 'A blind man's memory for voices is keener than any other's is for a face.'

'When did I come?' I asked.

'Immediately after Herr Etherage, when he commissioned the stick which you have in your possession. You said that you wanted a revolver, and had come to the wrong sort of establishment. I could hear the pretence in your tone.'

'I congratulate you, Herr von Herder, while sympathizing over the condition which has caused you to develop this remarkable faculty.'

'Acid,' he said. 'Etching a shotgun barrel when I was a careless youth. What can I do for you, Herr . . . Mauerstein, wasn't it? I hope your friend Herr Schmidt is keeping well.'

I detected obvious relief at my friendly approach. Having laughed at his quip, I said, still speaking lightly, 'I believe that the late Herr Professor Moriarty was a customer of yours.'

He said nothing, so I continued, leaning a little towards him and hardening my tone.

'Why did you betray him?'

'Betray? What is this?'

'You told his whereabouts to someone who came asking for them.'

'Nonsense! Yes, the Herr Professor Moriarty was a customer of mine several years ago. He has been dead now three years, perhaps. There was some report of an accident in Switzerland.'

'Herr von Herder, I think it was a mistake to reveal your little display of virtuosity just now. You recognized my voice, which you heard only once before in your life. That tells me that when Herr Etherage came here to commission this cane, you would have known at once whom he really was. Even I could have recognized that voice anywhere, and I'm not blind.'

'I . . . I . . . I was surprised. I confess there was something very similar to the Herr Professor Moriarty's voice. But I knew that he was dead, so it could not have been he.'

'You didn't ask him?'

'Certainly not!' He tried to retrieve his position by a show of indignation. 'My business is one of great discretion. If a gentleman gives his name as Etherage, or Schmidt – or Mauerstein – he has his reasons, which I respect.'

'But you were surprised how similar Etherage's voice was to Moriarty's which was so distinctive?'

'Very surprised. But it was not possible.'

'When Herr Etherage's cane was ready for collection, you ordered your assistant to write to him at Karlsruhe, asking him to come and collect it?'

'That is so.'

'And the man who came – was he the same?'

'Herr Etherage in person. Of course. I should not have handed it over to anyone else.'

'The voice was exactly the same.'

'Of course.'

'Still uncannily like the late Moriarty's.'

'Yes. But, as I say, I knew it could not be.'

'But you must have thought about it a good deal between the two visits. After the first, you must surely have said to yourself, "If I had not heard that Professor Moriarty was killed in that accident in Switzerland, I'd have sworn that it was he who has just ordered this new stick-gun. He spoke quite familiarly to me. He has obviously been here before. He knows my business procedures, etc. But no, it can't be. Moriarty is dead." Didn't you think at all along those lines?'

'I may have done. Yes, perhaps I did.'

'So when Etherage came again, you would be listening all the more intently to him, trying to convince yourself that he couldn't possibly be the late lamented Moriarty even though the voice sounded so similar.'

'Well, maybe you're right. But what is the purpose of all these questions? You come here with Herr Etherage's cane, on some errand you won't explain. You question me about Professor Moriarty, who is dead...'

'Yes, von Herder, Professor Moriarty is dead. He was shot to death a few days ago with the very air-rifle which you made for him several years ago.'

Amazement and incomprehension were blended in the man's features, despite the expressionlessness of his blind eyes.

'Then . . . then why . . . I am sorry. I cannot understand.'

'When Professor Moriarty ordered the special air-rifle he did not intend it to be for his own use. He was not a marksman. He ordered it for a colleague, whose name I think you may know.'

'I don't believe . . .'

'Try hard,' I ordered, putting on fresh menace. I twisted the lion's head of the stick. The concealed mechanism sprang out. The sound of it was all too obvious to von Herder.

'A Colonel Moran,' he hastened to answer. 'He came here with the Herr Professor, to try the balance of the weapon for himself.'

'And he has been back recently. The truth, von Herder.'

'Yes, yes. He was passing through Munich, and decided to bring the weapon for an overhaul. I recommend all purchasers of specially-made guns to return them to me from time to time.'

'When did he come?'

'Some little time after Herr Etherage took delivery of the cane which you now have. A few weeks later, perhaps.'

'Are you sure that it was purely a chance visit?'

'Positive. He had been in Africa for almost a year, and was afraid lest the climate should have affected the mechanism in any way. I was able to test it while he waited, and found it in perfect order.'

'And while he waited, you chatted together.'

'Naturally.'

'Of the late Moriarty.'

'His lamented death was mentioned, of course.'

'And you told Moran how curious it was that a customer whose voice was indistinguishable from Moriarty's had recently ordered a stick-gun from you.'

'Yes, yes. That was it. Just like that. I never said that I suspected that he really had been the Herr Professor in person.'

'Although that was what you had come to suspect.'

'I . . . I was fairly well convinced of it. I have been blind for so long. My hearing is acute to the least nuance in a voice.'

'So, what nuance did you pick up from Moran's reaction to what you had told him?'

'He made no disguise of his interest in what I had said. He questioned me as keenly as you yourself are doing.'

'To the point of asking for this other customer's name and address?'

'I declined to give it, though. I told him he should understand that it is against all my principles to make disclosures.'

'And what then?'

'I heard him turning the pages of my ledger but, of course, there were many entries, so it could tell him nothing. Then he . . . he came close to me, and placed a revolver against my side, and said he would shoot me if I would not give him the information. I still tried to resist, Herr . . . Herr Mauerstein. He said he would count to three . . .'

'And you gave in. You told him the name Etherage, and he was able to find the address in the ledger.'

'I swear that was how it was. There was no betrayal. How could there be? I see now that I was foolish to have mentioned the similarity of the voices at all – but how was I to know? It was mere gossip, to pass the time.'

He heard me return the stick-gun's mechanism to its concealment, and his thin old shoulders sagged with relief.

'What is the truth, Herr Mauerstein?' he begged. 'Please tell me what I am to believe?'

'The truth, Herr von Herder, is that your Herr Etherage was indeed Professor Moriarty. His death in Switzerland was a deception, but you can take it from me that he is now truly dead. I am a police agent investigating his murder, which was carried out with a soft-nosed revolver bullet, fired at high velocity, from a distance which rules out a revolver. Witnesses report hearing no shot. The obvious conclusion is that the weapon was the air-rifle made by you to Moriarty's order for his friend and colleague in crime, Moran. It was to get away from Moran that Moriarty faked his accidental death. He might still be alive now, if Moran had not come here, over two years later, and learned from you that he had never died at all.'

'As God is my judge, it emerged just as I have described. I understood that the two were friends. I should have made no mention of the Professor's visits here if I had known that Moran was pursuing him.'

'The irony of it is that he was almost certainly not pursuing him at that time. He had genuinely given him up for dead. It was your chance gossip which made him suspicious.'

The old gunsmith rubbed his head helplessly.

199

'I have long since learned to come to terms with my blindness. Now you remind me what an accursed handicap it is. I have been blind in more ways than one.'

'Do not trouble your conscience further. I accused you of betraying the Professor in order to shock and frighten you, and make you tell me the truth, which I believe you have done.'

'I swear it, sir.'

'You said nothing to Colonel Moran of my own visit here?'

'Definitely not. I had no reason to connect you with Herr Etherage . . . Moriarty.'

'Good. I see from Colonel Moran's entry in your ledger that he came here some two weeks after the date on which I happen to know Professor Moriarty finally left his Karlsruhe address, otherwise he would certainly have attacked him there. However, your information confirms that I am on the track of the right man, which was my purpose in coming here. I caution you, Herr von Herder, that if Colonel Moran should come back here, you will say nothing of my visit, or of what I have told you today. Should you do so, I am certain to learn of it, and you will find yourself facing charges concerning the manufacture and supply of a weapon which has been used for murder.'

'I swear to God, sir. The Herr Professor Moriarty was my customer, not Colonel Moran, and my first loyalty is to him.'

'Your scruples do you credit, Herr von Herder, though not everyone would say the same of the nature of your trade. Every man to his own business and his own conscience, though. I bid you good day.'

'Good day, Herr . . . Mauerstein.'

I went from Munich to Karlsruhe, secure in my altered appearance. A carefully framed inquiry at the old lodgings, where I was not recognized, confirmed that an Englishman, who had not given his name, but whose description matched Moran's, had indeed called there seeking Herr Etherage, who by then had left, giving no forwarding address.

So the trail had grown cold for Moran at that point, as it had now done for me. I could only return to London, lie low, and wait for him to show up.

Instead, a sudden idea took me to France – to Grenoble, in point of fact. There I called upon an old acquaintance, Monsieur Oscar Meunier, whom I knew to be as great an artist at wax sculpture as August von Herder was at making guns.

DEATH AND RESURRECTION

WATSON HAS supplied most of the details of what followed, in his admirable narrative entitled *The Empty House*, whose tidings of my 'return to life' gladdened his readers' hearts, while unwittingly providing them with a pack of lies.

In all my life I have never met a truer, less devious man than Watson, and I am aware of the affection in which he is held by his literary public, who compare favourably the modest self-portrait which emerges from his writings with the portrayal which he persisted in giving of myself as something half-human, half-automaton. Yet, seldom can a biographer have foisted upon his public more lies than Watson upon his. He should be absolved from all blame, though. In chronicling what became of me and Moriarty at the Reichenbach Falls, and subsequently correcting that record, he was acting as the victim of double deception upon himself. He told that which he was manipulated into telling and – unless he concealed it, of which I should not have thought him capable – never suspected that he had been deceived and lied to from start to finish.

Having told the true story at last, I had better round it off. In many respects, Watson's version is correct. It is in certain incidental particulars and omissions that, through no fault or design of his, he goes astray.

My stay in Grenoble lasted a week. My old friend Meunier, who had connections with my Vernet ancestors, did not exactly faint (as Watson was subsequently to do) on my removing my disguise in the privacy of his parlour, but he spent some time upbraiding me for having brought him to the verge of apoplexy. When he had regained his wits, I gave him a brief and wholly untrue account of how I had escaped death and where I had been for three years. Then I asked if I might stay in his house, unidentified to his servants, for as long as it would take him to model a life-size head and shoulders bust of me.

Part of Grenoble in southeast France where I spent a week with my old friend Oscar Meunier while he modelled the lifesize head and shoulders bust of me which I used to draw Colonel Sebastian Moran into the open.

He consented with delight, and we spent a jolly week while he worked and we talked and drank much red wine. Despite himself, he could not help plying me with questions which proved a useful exercise, for it enabled me to formulate that glibly false account of my wanderings which, for all the discrepancies that I have since recognized in it, I was to be able to foist onto Watson as the 'authorized version'.

I resumed my disguise and travelled to London, with Meunier's excellent creation in my baggage. It stands in a corner of this parlour now, on a low plinth. My opinion of people who hang portraits of themselves in their houses has never been approving, but the wax bust is my one personal concession to the practice. It is not here from vanity, or I should have asked Meunier subsequently to repair the ravages made by the bullet passing through the head. Only by leaving it in that damaged state could I have justified keeping it on view.

Mycroft received me in his own Pall Mall rooms this time, and listened to my plan.

'Admirable, Sherlock,' he said at last. 'You can hide away here. Our own people and the police are keeping a sharp watch for Moran. He hasn't shown himself yet, but I believe it is only a matter of time. It will be no trouble to contrive a means whereby he accidentally learns that you are alive after all, and back in London yourself. Then let us hope the rest goes as you intend.'

It has always been among my regrets that another life had to be forfeited before this matter was settled. Watson has the details of how the young Honourable Robert Adair had the misfortune to get into a whist game at the Bagatelle Card Club in the evening of 30 March 1894 as one of a foursome who included Colonel Sebastian Moran. How Moran entered the club without being seen by the constable on watch there for him, I have never known, but there are constables and constables, and always have been and always will. Perhaps, to do the man justice, Moran had been lodging on the club premises; but at least there was a missed chance for him to be seen when he left them later that evening, to follow young Adair to the house at 427 Park Lane, where he was living with his mother and sister, and shoot him through the open window of his room, high up in the house.

As soon as I read the details of the murder – a soft-nosed revolver bullet, which had shattered the youth's head, but no report of any shot being heard, and all the signs pointing to its having been fired from a distance and angle at which no revolver could have been so accurately used – I knew that Moran was responsible. There, indeed, was his name, as one of Adair's card partners that evening, and his quoted response to the newspaper's reporter: 'A dastardly deed. He left the club in excellent spirits, after winning modestly. The Empire cannot afford to lose such fine young fellows.'

'Tragic!' Mycroft exclaimed. 'Of course, they're looking for some scandal, but he seems to have been a thoroughly decent, clean-living, honourable chap.'

'Too honourable for Moran, perhaps,' I said. 'What are the odds that young Adair spotted him at his cheating again, and threatened to expose him? It would have finished him in his clubs, as it did in the army. Perhaps he gave Moran twenty-four hours or so in which to resign of his own accord. If so, it was tantamount to signing his own death warrant.'

'Well, it has flushed out Moran. Are you ready to act?'

'Without delay. Please bring Lestrade here yourself, Mycroft. Say, five o'clock. Better prepare him for the shock. Meanwhile, I will step round to Baker Street and reduce the good Mrs Hudson to hysterics.'

I had adopted a fresh disguise now, as a seedy old bookseller, almost hunchbacked, with a wizened face and white side-whiskers. A shabby suit completed the effect. When I shuffled away from Mycroft's premises I bore in one hand a few old volumes, and in the other an ancient gladstone bag, in which lay Meunier's bust of myself.

Mrs Hudson's indignant attempt to reject me at her front door occasioned nothing in the way of noise compared with her reaction when I spoke to her in my own voice, addressing her by name. I bundled her hastily indoors, out of sight and hearing, and spent as long as it took to convince her that I was neither withered corpse, ghost, nor anything but myself in disguise and in need of her help.

In the sitting room, preserved just as I remembered it, and redolent of happy memories, we kept well clear of the window as we set up the revolving Lazy Betty on which so many joints had been carved for Watson and myself in the good old days. We placed it on a low table under the window, so that the bust, when standing on it, would appear in perfect silhouette from the empty house across the road, which I was convinced an expert such as Moran would choose as his natural firing point.

'Wait until it is time to light the lamps, Mrs Hudson,' I instructed. 'Pull down the blind first, then put the bust in place, and only then light the lamps – in that order, you understand?'

'Aye, Mr Holmes.'

Park Lane, one of London's most fashionable thoroughfares. It was through an open window of his mother's rented mansion, No. 427, in March 1894, that the Hon. Ronald Adair was shot through the head by Col. Sebastian Moran from across the road in Hyde Park.

205

'Oh, and drape one of my old dressing gowns about the bust's shoulders before you light up. Then anyone watching from the street won't see you meddling with the bust. There will just be my outline on the blind.'

'How often shall I turn it, sir?'

'Not too often. Its attitude makes it appear that I am sitting reading. I should not be likely to move about much, but even a reader shifts his position occasionally. Whatever you do, when you turn the Lazy Betty, stay on your hands and knees.'

'I'll no' let my shadow show,' she promised.

'Not only that. Unless I'm in for a disappointment, a bullet is going to be put through that head before this evening is out, and there will be glass flying. Since I propose to move back into residence at the first opportunity, I prefer you to remain intact for my happy homecoming.'

'Awa' with ye, Mr Holmes! Still making fun. Will the Doctor be coming back, too, puir man?'

The wax bust of me made at Grenoble by Oscar Meunier. The bullet put through its head by Colonel Sebastian Moran on the night of 5 April 1894 was intended for me – as I had planned it should be. The details are recorded in THE EMPTY HOUSE.

'I hope so, Mrs Hudson. If I have learned anything in these past three years, it is that one should recognize when one is comfortable and ideally situated, and who are one's truest friends. If you ever hear me complaining again, you have leave to scold me.'

'Awa'! Ye'll aye complain, when the boredom's on ye. I'll be glad to be hearin' ye at it again, Mr Holmes.'

I took my leave, hoping soon to resume permanent residence without delay. Inspector Lestrade, as lean and ratty-looking as ever, was awaiting me at Mycroft's.

'Come back to make my life a misery again, have you, Mr Holmes?' he grinned, pumping my hand nevertheless. 'Just when I was reckoning how smoothly everything was going, without you around to turn my inquiries on their heads.'

'Just looked in to solve this Adair tragedy for you, Lestrade. Incidentally, you may not know it, but tonight's little event, if it goes well, will mark the true end of the Moriarty gang.'

'What? I thought we had all of them long ago.'

'All bar the most vicious scoundrel of the lot. But we'll have him tonight – by the Lord Harry we shall!'

And as Watson relates, have him we did. Mycroft had, by one of his mysterious means, conveyed a hint to Moran through a fellow clubman that Sherlock Holmes was alive and back in London, personally investigating the Adair murder at the bereaved family's request. That was how we lured him to the empty house in Baker Street, where he saw my silhouette against the window blind, and saw it move in lifelike fashion when Mrs Hudson gave a little turn to the Lazy Betty. As I had predicted, with his air-rifle he put a bullet through the head of that wax bust which is now a reminder of my features in younger days. But our ambush was set, and we had him.

Under natural justice, Colonel Sebastian Moran should have gone to the gallows. In the event, he did not. The science of ballistics had not yet been evolved in 1894. What would, within a matter of years, have become the commonplace course of comparing the bullet which he fired through my waxen head with the fragments of that which had exploded inside the head of poor young Adair, was then an undiscovered technique. On its own, his shooting of Adair could not be proved beyond all reasonable doubt. As to his attempt on me, a man who, to all intents and purposes, was already dead – that posed numerous complications, especially since he had not shot me, but at a mere waxen image of me. In any case, mention of me in connection with him was undesirable, as was any reference to Moriarty's killing. Too many questions would have arisen, both in court and in the press, for the authorities' comfort.

Mycroft therefore arranged for a deal to be done with Moran whereby his sentence would be one of imprisonment only if he would plead guilty to one of his past crimes. The one redeeming feature about Moran was that he was a staunch patriot, and did not insist on disclosing what he knew of Moriarty's survival of Reichenbach. I never did learn how he had tracked Moriarty to Portland; and the relative lightness of the sentence left me with a feeling that Moriarty had gone less thoroughly avenged than I had wished, not to mention poor young Adair.

My consolation which overrode all this was to have been reunited with Watson – indeed, to have had him at my side when Moran was taken in the act. He himself has told more graphically than ever I could of his blundering in the street into a bent old bookseller who insisted on calling on him afterwards, how the old man had distracted his attention for a moment, and then:

> When I turned again Sherlock Holmes was standing smiling at me across my study table. I rose to my feet, stared at him for some seconds in utter amazement, and then it appears that I must have fainted for the first and the last time in my life. Certainly a grey mist swirled before my eyes, and when it cleared I found my collar-ends undone and the tingling after-taste of brandy upon my lips. Holmes was bending over my chair, his flask in his hand.
>
> 'My dear Watson,' said the well-remembered voice, 'I owe you a thousand apologies. I had no idea that you would be so affected.'
>
> I gripped him by the arm.
>
> 'Holmes!' I cried. 'Is it really you? Can it indeed be that you are alive? Is it possible that you succeeded in climbing out of that awful abyss?'

That was the point at which the so-termed Great Hiatus became the Great Lie.